Time to Eat

'No clock is more regular than the belly.'
Francois Rabelais (1494–1553),
taken from works, 1V

10/18 DATE DUE FOR RETURN

Renewals
www.liverpool.gov.uk/libraries
0151 233 3000

R.267

Time to Eat

Gary Rhodes

Photography by Lottie Davies

Michael Joseph
an imprint of Penguin Books

This gentleman has stood by me for fifteen years.
He is one of so few who gives 100% dedication to the culinary
world. With his loyalty and support, he has allowed me the time
and space to develop the career I have so much enjoyed.

As a token of recognition for these past fifteen years,
I dedicate this book to Wayne Tapsfield, with my thanks.

MICHAEL JOSEPH

Published by the Penguin Group
Penguin Books Ltd, 80 Strand, London WC2R 0RL, England
Penguin Group (USA) Inc., 375 Hudson Street, New York, New York 10014, USA
Penguin Group (Canada), 90 Eglinton Avenue East, Suite 700, Toronto, Ontario, Canada M4P 2Y3
(a division of Pearson Penguin Canada Inc.)
Penguin Ireland, 25 St Stephen's Green, Dublin 2, Ireland (a division of Penguin Books Ltd)
Penguin Group (Australia), 250 Camberwell Road,
Camberwell, Victoria 3124, Australia (a division of Pearson Australia Group Pty Ltd)
Penguin Books India Pvt Ltd, 11 Community Centre,
Panchsheel Park, New Delhi – 110 017, India
Penguin Group (NZ), 67 Apollo Drive, Rosedale, North Shore 0632, New Zealand
(a division of Pearson New Zealand Ltd)
Penguin Books (South Africa) (Pty) Ltd, 24 Sturdee Avenue,
Rosebank, Johannesburg 2196, South Africa

Penguin Books Ltd, Registered Offices: 80 Strand, London WC2R 0RL, England

www.penguin.com

First published 2007

1

Printed in Great Britain by Butler and Tanner, Frome, Somerset
Colour Reproduction by Dot Gradations Ltd, Essex
A CIP catalogue record for this book is available from the British Library

ISBN: 978–0–718–15314–4

contents

introduction

Why does it seem that we repeat the same, oh so familiar, nightmare when we're having friends round for dinner? Our day begins so well at the supermarket or, even better, our local market, shopping list in hand, hunting down the freshest of produce for our chosen recipes. Only to find, of course, that the essential ingredient is all sold out. Meanwhile, our partner decides to go wine hunting and is never seen again (reappearing late afternoon with the excuse that tasting and decision-making took some time, but, unlike you, still somehow having found time for a light lunch!).

As the day progresses, the preparation begins. Some organized people earn top brownie points, but most just hope for the best and for everyone, time is running out. It's already 6 pm and it should be shower and dressing time, but it seems your partner is still checking that wine, having failed to lay the table as planned. Once you've sped through your own jobs and are finally ready, it's straight back to work, apron on and a return to the stoves, extra perfume or aftershave advisable to cover up that onion odour.

At 7.30 pm, the doorbell rings and it's apron off, smile on and to the door. Champagne, wine or whatever is poured and the evening begins, well it does for your guests – you're heading back to the kitchen. Once you've all sat down you can finally begin to relax, but do we ever really enjoy the whole experience?

We're certainly pleased at all the smiles and the positive comments about the food, but in our heads – never again. All of this has happened to me many a time, a professional chef finding that without a restaurant kitchen (and brigade), things are just that little bit more difficult.

Hence, *Time to Eat*. Obviously, I don't have people round every day and not every dish I cook is for a special dinner, but time is still often a pressure. Getting your timing right in the kitchen is the best way to ensure you produce wonderful everyday or dinner party food that exceeds your expectations without raising your blood pressure. As each chapter follows the one before, the cooking time increases, starting from absolutely nothing in 'No time to cook' right the way through to 'Proper puddings – worth every minute', where fantastic flavour, not time, is of the essence. The book allows you to be totally in command of your own time, with different types of ingredients and styles of cooking chosen to suit the time available.

You'll also find that simplicity, as with my previous book *Keeping it Simple*, is the overall concept behind my recipes here. It's all about returning pleasure to the kitchen for both parties: the cook and the diners. Many of the recipes have fewer than four or five ingredients (not including, of course, the basics such as oils, butter and seasonings) and there are often even less stages of preparation and cooking.

As with all my cooking, I do stress that I present these recipes to you purely as guidelines, ones that reflect my own favourite flavours and decisions. With so many wonderful ingredients now available to us, use that freedom to give your food its own character and personality on the plate.

Now, it's *Time to Eat*.

cook's notes

Butter Like most chefs, I generally use unsalted butter when I'm cooking to give me total control over the seasoning. However, this is not essential, so use whatever you have.

Eggs All the eggs I use are free range.

Fish Most fish you buy these days have already been prepared, scaled and often filleted. However, if I buy fillets, I do quickly check that the fine pin bones have been removed. Run your hand along a fillet and take out any stray bones with tweezers.

To devein prawns, cut down the back of the prawns using a sharp knife and remove the thin digestive tract. To butterfly them, cut slightly deeper to open up the backs.

For crab, always do a quick second check of picked crabmeat with your fingertips to remove any splinters of shell.

Oven temperatures I have given these in Celsius, Fahrenheit and a gas mark for all the recipes, but if you want to use your fan oven, check your manufacturer's recommendations before referring to my conversion table below to set the right temperature:

140°C	275°F	fan oven 120°C	gas 1	200°C	400°F	fan oven 180°C	gas 6
150°C	300°F	fan oven 130°C	gas 2	220°C	425°F	fan oven 200°C	gas 7
160°C	325°F	fan oven 140°C	gas 3	230°C	450°F	fan oven 210°C	gas 8
180°C	350°F	fan oven 160°C	gas 4	240°C	475°F	fan oven 220°C	gas 9
190°C	375°F	fan oven 170°C	gas 5				

Salt and pepper I use both coarse sea salt and table salt in my cooking. I also prefer the taste and texture of white pepper to black, but use whatever you prefer.

Stocks Home-made stock is lovely, but it's certainly not quick and simple to make, and these days there are lots of instant varieties on offer. Try one of the tubs of liquid stocks available in the chilled cabinets or a tin of consommé, which provides the richest of flavours. Beef is the easiest to get hold of and it suits most meat and chicken dishes, while game consommé is the one to use for game dishes and duck. If you're making your stock using cubes, look for the rectangular ones with a paste-like texture, rather than the crumbly cubes, and add just half a cube to the recommended water quantity for a fresher, less artificial flavour. For a clear finish, boil the water in a saucepan, whisk in the cube and simmer for 1 to 2 minutes to clarify.

Tomatoes To remove the skins from tomatoes for a smooth finish to your sauce or soup you will need to blanch them. Remove the eye with the point of a sharp knife and cut a cross in the opposite end. Plunge into boiling water for 10 to 15 seconds before plunging into iced water. Once cold, the skins peel away easily.

no time to shop

no time to shop

Being short of time to shop doesn't have to spell takeaway. Resist and open your fridge again. Most kitchens are in fact bursting with food: tins and opened packets, a carrot, half an onion, some eggs. Amongst all this, I promise you, is a delicious meal, you just need to find it.

Treat your bare cupboards as a challenge and a chance to revisit old friends. That polenta at the back needs only a knob of butter and a sprinkle of Parmesan to bring it to life, while that pack of mushrooms could be grilled with onions and cheese and be bubbling on your table in under 15 minutes. Being intuitive and creative with whatever ingredients you have to hand is the essence of great, simple cooking.

If your life is always busy, just a few permanent additions to your weekly shopping list will ensure you always have dinner. My kitchen is never without:

Oil and butter You'll need these two if you're going to do pretty much any cooking at all.

Eggs Probably the most useful of ingredients and one that combines with almost any savoury produce you can find to make an omelette or frittata.

Cheese If you have eggs and cheese, your hunt is over, you have a meal already. My fridge is never without Cheddar and Parmesan.

Pasta Try to think like an Italian and keep it simple. Capers, olives, dried chilli flakes, anchovies, lemon, a tin of tomatoes, Parmesan and olive oil are all fabulous additions to pasta and are probably in your kitchen already.

Sausages or minced beef This is what your freezer is for, not an icy waiting room for ready meals but to store sausages or minced beef that can quickly be turned into dinner.

Onions and garlic These provide the essential flavour and savoury base for so many dishes.

Bacon I always have a pack in my fridge.

A tin of chopped tomatoes Not just for quick pasta sauces, but also to thicken and add flavour to soups and one pots.

spicy potato soup

Warm the oil and butter together in a saucepan and add the chopped onion. Cover with a lid and cook over a medium heat for a few minutes before adding the curry powder.

Add the potato and continue to cook for a further 5 to 10 minutes.

Pour the milk and 500ml (12fl oz) water over the potatoes and sprinkle in the vegetable stock cube. Bring to a simmer and cook for 15 to 20 minutes until the potatoes are completely tender. Season with a pinch of salt and blitz in a blender until smooth.

For a slightly sweet touch to the spicy flavour, add the mango chutney, a teaspoon at a time to suit your taste, liquidizing until smooth.

Divide the soup into bowls, finishing with the coriander leaves if you have them.

more
- *Crusty bread, poppadums or naan bread are perfect for dipping.*
- *The mango chutney can be omitted from the soup and instead a dollop or two spooned on top once served.*
- *100ml (4fl oz) of the stock or milk can be replaced with single cream for a richer soup.*

serves four–six

2 tablespoons sunflower or groundnut oil
a knob of butter
1 large onion, chopped
1 tablespoon medium curry powder
2 large jacket potatoes, peeled and cut into roughly 1cm (½ inch) cubes
500ml (12fl oz) milk
1 vegetable stock cube (see note on page 8)
salt
1–2 teaspoons mango chutney (optional)
1 tablespoon picked coriander leaves (if available)

tomato soup, spaghetti and meatballs

This recipe belongs to my wife, Jennie. It's become a household favourite, using up all our spare tomatoes and perhaps a sweet pepper with some dried spaghetti and a pack of mince or sausages. Measurements are made by assumption and as for flavour, it's packed. The soup can be left chunky, but we prefer it blitzed and smooth.

Warm a saucepan with the olive oil. Add the sliced onion and cook over a medium heat until softened. Add the chilli powder and cook for a further couple of minutes before stirring in the chopped pepper and fresh tomatoes. Continue to cook and, once beginning to soften, add the tinned tomatoes, loosening with 600ml (1 pint) of the chicken stock and returning to a simmer for 20 to 25 minutes over a gentle heat.

Meanwhile, warm the remaining chicken stock in a large saucepan until simmering.

Peel the sausages or season the mince and stir in the egg. Shape the sausage or beef mince into Malteser-sized balls. As you shape, drop them into the remainder of the simmering stock to poach and warm gently for just 10 minutes. They now have a succulent tenderness rather than a crispy fried chewy taste.

Snap the dried spaghetti into a large pan of boiling salted water and cook following the packet cooking time until tender but leaving a slight bite, then drain.

While cooking the pasta, the soup can be ladled into a blender and whizzed until smooth (or leave it rustic and chunky), loosening with the warmed chicken stock if needed (the soup is far heartier if left quite thick). Check for seasoning.

Stir the pasta and the meatballs as they are ready into the soup and serve.

serves four

2 tablespoons olive oil
2 onions, sliced
¼ teaspoon chilli powder or 1 deseeded and chopped fresh red chilli
1 red pepper, roughly chopped (not essential)
600g (1lb 5oz) tomatoes, quartered (however many you have)
400g (14oz) tin of chopped tomatoes
1–1.2 litres (1¾–2 pints) chicken stock (see note on page 8)
450g (1lb) pack of mince or sausages
salt and pepper
1 egg, if using mince
¼ packet dried spaghetti, snapped into 5cm (2 inch) pieces
lots of crusty bread, for dipping

sage and onion porkies

This is a very quick version of an old favourite of mine – a classic combination of pork with sage and onion. It's simply pork sausages, a packet of sage and onion stuffing and one egg. Once bound with the egg, the sausages are shaped into burgers and fried. Leftover mash or new potatoes sautéed in butter with fresh vegetables or frozen peas help create a full meal. Alternatively, place in a roll or between two slices of bread for a supper snack.

Cut and remove the skin from the sausages, placing the meat in a bowl. Stir in the sage and onion stuffing and egg, seasoning with salt and pepper. The mixture can now be divided into four and shaped as burgers.

Heat 2 tablespoons of the cooking oil in a large frying pan before placing in the porkies. Pan-fry over a medium heat for 5 to 6 minutes on each side until cooked through. The sage and onion porkies are now ready to eat.

more
- *A coarsely grated apple can be added to the mix, giving a fruity edge.*
- *This recipe also creates easy canapés. Simply roll the mixture into small balls and pan-fry before piercing with cocktail sticks. Smooth apple sauce or a flavoured mayonnaise are tasty dips to accompany.*

serves four

450g (1lb) pork sausages
85g (3½oz) packet of dried
  sage and onion stuffing
1 egg
salt and pepper
sunflower or vegetable oil,
  for cooking

ham, cheese and onion spaghetti

It's not essential to make this dish using spaghetti. More or less any shape of pasta can be used, basically whatever happens to be sitting in the cupboard. I've chosen Parmesan as the featured cheese here because it's the one I always have at home ready for grating over dishes, but so many other cheeses can be used, with Cheddar or Gorgonzola particular favourites.

Cook the spaghetti in boiling salted water until tender but leaving a slight bite, then drain.

Meanwhile, melt half the butter in a large frying pan and gently cook the grated onion until softened.

Add a few tablespoons of water along with the ham. Once warmed, stir in the rest of the butter to create a sauce consistency.

Add the cooked pasta and season with salt and pepper.

Stir in half the Parmesan and drizzle liberally with the olive oil, offering the remaining Parmesan to sprinkle over the top.

more
- *Tomatoes can also be added to this recipe, just half and deseed before chopping.*

serves four

400g (14oz) spaghetti
50g (2oz) butter
1 onion, grated (thinly sliced spring onions could also be used)
6–8 slices (approximately 200g/7oz) of ham, torn or chopped
salt and pepper
100g (4oz) Parmesan cheese, grated
olive oil, for drizzling

honey-mustard sausage bruschettas

English, Dijon or wholegrain mustard can all be used for this recipe. As for the bread, ciabatta is an obvious first choice, but a thick slice of bloomer or French baguette come a close second. Tossed green leaves are the simplest of accompaniments.

Warm 2 tablespoons of the oil in a frying pan, add the sausages and pan-fry for 10 to 15 minutes over a medium heat until golden brown on all sides and firm to the touch. For a slightly bitter taste, increase the heat, allowing the sausages to almost burn.

In a separate pan, fry the onion in a drizzle of oil and the knob of butter until softened and a rich golden brown. Season with salt and pepper.

Meanwhile, the bread slices can be toasted, fried or cooked on a grill pan, leaving burnt tinges around the edges.

Using kitchen paper, mop away excess fat from the sausage frying pan before adding the mustard and honey. Roll the sausages in the pan, allowing each to become well coated in the honey and mustard and remove from the heat.

Arrange the sausages on the bruschettas, spooning the onion on top.

more
• *The onions can be fried in the same pan as the sausages, adding the mustard and honey to create a completely sticky finish.*

serves four

vegetable oil, for cooking
450g (1lb) sausages
1 large onion, sliced
a knob of butter
salt and pepper
4 thick slices of bread
   (see left), drizzled with olive
   oil
2 tablespoons mustard
   (see left)
4 tablespoons clear honey

bacon and onion potatoes

An easy supper dish.

Cook the potatoes in their skins in boiling salted water for about 20 to 25 minutes until tender. Drain and roughly chop or break into bite-sized chunks.

Meanwhile, fry the bacon pieces in a very hot pan for a few minutes before stirring in the onion with a few tablespoons of olive oil. Cook until lightly coloured and softened.

In a large bowl, mix together the potatoes and fried bacon and onion, seasoning with salt and pepper before serving.

more
There are plenty of possible additions:
- *chopped tomatoes*
- *sliced mushrooms*
- *chopped herbs*
- *a fried egg on top*
- *a topping of salad leaves with a trickle of balsamic vinegar*

serves four

4–5 large potatoes or 1kg (2¼lb) new potatoes
6–8 rashers of streaky or back bacon, roughly chopped
3 onions, sliced
olive oil, for cooking
salt and pepper

bacon and egg risotto

Risotto should be made with Arborio, Carnaroli or Vialone nano rice (often listed as risotto rice on the packet), though if you only have a basic long grain variety available, you'll still finish with a moist and flavoursome braised rice dish.

Heat the olive oil and half the butter in a large shallow saucepan or deep frying pan. Add the onion and bacon and lightly fry for 6 to 8 minutes. Meanwhile, heat the stock in a separate saucepan until just simmering.

Over a gentle heat, add the rice to the onion and bacon and stir for a minute, allowing the rice to be coated with the butter without colouring.

Add a ladleful or two of the simmering stock, stirring gently. Once the stock has been absorbed, add a further ladleful, stirring and adding more as it continues to be absorbed.

Continue this process for 15 to 18 minutes (some rice may take up to 20 minutes) at which point the rice should be tender and creamy, but still maintaining the slightest of bites.

Meanwhile, to poach the eggs, fill a large saucepan with water and bring to a rapid simmer.

Add the remaining butter and Parmesan cheese to the risotto, if using, and season. The risotto can now be left to rest with a lid on while the eggs are poached.

Whisk the rapidly simmering water in a circular motion, cracking the eggs into the centre (as the liquid spins, it pulls and sets the white around the yolks before the eggs reach the base of the pan). Poach the eggs for 3 to 3½ minutes.

The risotto can now be spooned into bowls, topping each with a warm poached egg and drizzling with a drop of olive oil.

serves four

olive oil, for cooking
75g (3oz) butter
1 onion, finely chopped
6–8 rashers of streaky or
    back bacon, cut into strips
    or cubes
1–1.2 litres (1¾–2 pints)
    chicken stock (see note
    on page 8)
350g (12oz) risotto rice (see
    left)
50g (2oz) Parmesan cheese,
    grated (optional)
salt and pepper
4 eggs

red wine and mushroom poached eggs on toast

Boil the red wine with the sugar in a small saucepan, simmering down by three-quarters to leave approximately 75ml (3fl oz).

Meanwhile, heat a frying pan with a small knob of the measured butter and once sizzling, add the sliced mushrooms and fry over a high heat until well coloured and tender. Season with salt and pepper. Whisk the remaining butter into the red wine sauce before pouring over the mushrooms. Keep warm to one side.

Preheat the grill and fill a large saucepan with water and bring to a rapid simmer.

Toast the bread on one side under the grill, turning the bread and spreading with butter before returning it to beneath the grill and toasting to a buttery, golden brown.

Whisk the rapidly simmering water in a circular motion, cracking the eggs into the centre (as the liquid spins, it pulls and sets the white around the yolks before the eggs reach the base of the pan). Poach the eggs for 3 to 4 minutes.

Arrange the eggs on the toasts, spooning the red wine mushrooms over the top.

more
- *If available, a sprinkling of chopped parsley adds extra flavour and colour.*

serves two

300ml (10fl oz) red wine
1 heaped teaspoon caster
  sugar
50g (2oz) butter, plus extra for
  spreading
1–2 handfuls of mushrooms
  (whatever you have), sliced
salt and pepper
2 thick slices of crusty bread
4 eggs

three-mustard honey potato salad

This salad tastes great on its own, but can also be lifted by binding with a few salad, watercress or fresh herb leaves and a sprinkling of shredded spring onion. The dressing is made from three mustards: wholegrain, Dijon and English. If you only keep one in house, wholegrain would be my first choice, the Dijon or English best added a teaspoon at a time to your liking. If you happen to have smoked salmon, prawns or ham, all are perfect accompaniments, or even just a warm poached egg or two.

Cook the new potatoes in boiling salted water for 20 to 25 minutes until tender. Drain and, while still warm, halve the potatoes. Season with salt and pepper.

Meanwhile, in a bowl whisk together the honey, vinegar and mustards followed by the olive oil. Season with salt and pepper.

Add the warm potatoes, mixing all together well to coat each potato. The salad is ready to serve.

more
- *If the vinegars are unavailable, lemon juice can be used in their place.*
- *A drizzling of crème fraîche or sour cream helps calm the mustard.*
- *The olive oil in the dressing can be replaced with 2 tablespoons walnut or hazelnut oil mixed with 1 tablespoon groundnut.*

serves four

900g (2lb) new potatoes
sea salt and pepper
1 tablespoon clear honey
1 tablespoon white wine or red wine vinegar
1 tablespoon wholegrain mustard
1 teaspoon Dijon mustard
½ teaspoon English mustard
4 tablespoons olive oil

open chip butty

The chips are home-made French fries, cooked for just 10 minutes or so and sitting upon a thick slice of crusty bread with mayonnaise or butter. If there are tomatoes, cucumber and spring onions in the fridge, a very quick salad can be put together as the potatoes fry. Skin left on the spuds or peeled off is personal choice.

Heat 4–5cm (1½–2 inches) of oil over a low heat in a wok or frying pan (a wok is good because it allows the oil to be deeper) until only just warm.

Cut the potatoes into long 5–6mm (¼ inch) thick sticks. Dry on kitchen paper and gently drop into the warm oil. Allow the oil to just simmer for 5 to 6 minutes until the potatoes have become tender without colouring. Once tender, increase the heat to maximum and continue to fry to a rich golden brown. Using a slotted spoon, lift the potatoes from the oil on to kitchen paper.

Meanwhile, spread mayonnaise or butter liberally over each slice of bread. Top with the French fries and season with sea salt.

serves two

vegetable oil, for frying
2 large or 3 medium potatoes
  (see left)
mayonnaise or butter, for
  spreading
2 thick slices of bread
sea salt

crispy quarter pounders

Does this fit in our 'no time to shop' chapter? On my home evidence it does because there's often a pack or two of lean minced beef sitting in the fridge. This recipe has taken a healthy approach to the burger with crispy iceberg lettuce replacing the baps and the burgers grilled with barely a brush of oil. There's garnish included: tomato, cucumber (quickly pickled), onion and a light mayonnaise flavoured with mustard (American is the first choice to go with the burger).

Mix together the minced beef and egg, seasoning with salt and pepper. Divide the mince into four, shaping and pressing each into a burger.

Heat a grill pan or the grill. Brush the burgers with the oil and cook for 6 to 7 minutes on each side (using a baking tray if beneath the grill) for medium.

Meanwhile, cut the cucumber into thick slices. Put the slices in a bowl and season with salt, pepper and a pinch of sugar. Add a small splash of malt vinegar and mix well.

Stir together the mayonnaise and the chosen mustard.

Present the burgers on the tomato slices, topping with the mustard mayonnaise, cucumber slices and onion rings. Finish with the burger on an iceberg leaf, topping with another leaf, if preferred.

more
- *A slice of Gruyère cheese can be melted over the burger.*

serves four

450g (1lb) lean minced beef
1 egg, beaten
salt and pepper
vegetable oil, for brushing
½ cucumber, peeled
a pinch of sugar
a dash of malt vinegar
4 tablespoons light
  mayonnaise
mustard, to taste (American,
  Dijon, English, wholegrain)
1 beef steak tomato cut into
  4 slices
1 onion (a red onion if
  available), sliced into rings
½ iceberg lettuce, divided
  into leaves

no time to cook

no time to cook

When you find yourself with no time to cook, your lead ingredient simply must have maximum flavour, which for fruit and vegetables usually means produce in season. Luckily, not only is summer the season when you most feel like downing kitchen tools, heading to the garden and enjoying a lightly dressed salad or paper-thin Parma ham, but nature obligingly provides an abundance of exceptional ingredients that need no cooking to enjoy: soft English salad leaves, sweet red peppers, cool cucumbers, bursting cherry tomatoes and pots of herbs.

I've included three dressings with my simple salad to inspire you to make the best of all those fresh ingredients, but if you think beyond the tomato and cucumber, you'll find many more vegetables that can be eaten without cooking. Tender baby or spring varieties, sliced very thin, add superb texture to salads. Courgette ribbons are the perfect partner for soft avocado in my avocado and courgette salad with lime vinaigrette, while asparagus and fennel, finely shaved on a mandolin, are delicious raw in mixed fennel, asparagus, grapefruit and apple.

Despite the treasure chest of vegetables to be enjoyed just picked, no cooking certainly doesn't have to mean no meat. A whole range of cured prosciuttos are now available in this country, not only Parma ham but San Daniele, French Bayonne and Spanish serrano hams, all of which now sit side by side with our fabulous British ham. Mix and match your own platter or look to my Italian inspired smoked duck with buffalo mozzarella, orange and lamb's lettuce or more French-leaning charcuterie board with celeriac, apple, pear and walnut coleslaw for ideas. For fish lovers, I've put together a platter of three smoked fish salads, smoked salmon, smoked trout, smoked mackerel, which would make an unusual dinner party starter, perfect for sharing.

If your thoughts are turning to dinner for friends, then a cold starter that can be plated up or arranged on a platter to share before your guests even arrive is always a clever choice. I think every recipe in this chapter would give you a stunning start to a special meal, and many of the dishes would suit a complete one course meal.

avocado and courgette salad with lime vinaigrette

Trim the ends of the courgettes and, with a Y-shaped potato peeler, slice lengthways into long, thin strips.

Whisk together the lime juice, olive oil and sugar, seasoning with salt and a twist of pepper before stirring in the chopped mint.

Add the avocado and courgette strips to the dressing. Gently fold in the rocket leaves before dividing the salad among plates or offering in a large bowl.

more
Here's a few extras to consider for this salad:
- *toasted pine nuts*
- *lime segments*
- *crispy iceberg leaves*

serves two–four

4 small or 2 medium
   courgettes
2 tablespoons lime juice
2 tablespoons olive oil
½ teaspoon caster sugar
sea salt and pepper
1 heaped teaspoon
   chopped mint
1 avocado, peeled and cut
   into 8 wedges
a large handful of rocket
   leaves

mixed leaves with melon, brie and parma ham

Cut the melon into eight wedges, scooping away the seeds and removing the skin. Chop each wedge into large chunks.

Whisk together the red wine vinegar and olive oil, seasoning with salt and a twist of pepper. In a bowl, mix together the salad leaves, melon chunks and just enough red wine dressing to coat.

Present the salad on a large platter or individual plates with the softened Brie slices, finishing with torn strips of Parma ham and any remaining dressing.

serves four

1 chilled Ogen or Charentais melon
2 tablespoons red wine vinegar
4 tablespoons olive oil (half walnut oil can also be used)
sea salt and pepper
200g (7oz) bag of washed mixed salad leaves
225g (8oz) room-temperature Brie, cut into 8 thin slices
8–12 slices of Parma ham

smoked duck with buffalo mozzarella, orange and lamb's lettuce

Blood oranges can also be used in this recipe, in season during our later winter and early spring months, offering a richer flavour and often shocking deep orange and red colour and juices. Italian cured ham, Prosciutto Crudo, is a good alternative to the duck, if preferred.

Top and tail the oranges. The rind and pith can now be removed by cutting in a sawing motion down the sides. To release the segments, cut between each membrane, saving all the juice.

Arrange the slices of smoked duck breast (remove the skin if preferred) and mozzarella on a large platter or individual plates, scattering with the orange segments and lamb's lettuce. Sprinkle with sea salt and a generous twist of black pepper.

Warm together the marmalade and a tablespoon of the saved orange juice (these can simply be microwaved together for 20 seconds).

Whisk in the olive oil with the juice and season with salt and pepper. Drizzle over the top of the platter and serve.

more
- *Thin slices of apple also work well with this salad, as do black olives.*

serves four

3 oranges
2 large smoked duck (5–6 slices per portion)
2 buffalo mozzarella, sliced or cut into chunks
100–150g/4–5oz bunch of lamb's lettuce, washed
sea salt and black pepper
2 tablespoons marmalade
4 tablespoons olive oil

smoked salmon, smoked trout, smoked mackerel

Three smoked fish and three salads. There's 50g (2oz) of each fish for a generous starter or lunch/supper dish.

For the smoked salmon, top and tail the grapefruit, slicing down following the natural shape of the fruit and removing all skin and pith. Cut between each membrane to release the segments. Divide each segment into three or four chunks. Stir the grapefruit pieces and avocado together in a small bowl with a few drops of the oil. Season with a generous twist of pepper and pinch of sea salt, topping with cress or rocket, if using. Arrange the slices of salmon on top or next to the salad.

For the smoked trout, stir together the vinegar and lemon juice in a small bowl, adding the two oils and whisking the vinaigrette slowly into the cream. Season with salt and pepper. Bind the little gem leaves with the dressing. Arrange the pieces of smoked trout on top or next to the salad.

For the smoked mackerel, in another small bowl stir together the chopped apple, sliced spring onion, sugar and vinegar. Stir in the torn pieces of smoked mackerel, adding enough cream to bind. Season with salt and pepper.

Present the three smoked fish salads on plates.

serves four as a starter

for the smoked salmon
1 grapefruit
1 large avocado, peeled and chopped
a few drops of olive oil
sea salt and pepper
sprigs of baby watercress, mustard cress or rocket (optional)
225g (8oz) sliced smoked salmon

for the smoked trout
1 teaspoon white wine vinegar
1 tablespoon lemon juice
1 tablespoon groundnut or grape seed oil
3 tablespoons hazelnut oil
3 tablespoons double cream or crème fraîche
sea salt and pepper
1 little gem, leaves separated
2 smoked trout fillets, each cut into 4 neat pieces

for the smoked mackerel
1 apple, quartered and chopped
1 spring onion, peeled and thinly sliced
¼ teaspoon caster sugar
2 teaspoons cider vinegar
225g (8oz) smoked mackerel fillet, broken into bite-sized pieces
2–3 tablespoons sour cream
salt and pepper

cherry tomato gems

Whisk together the quartered cherry tomatoes and olive oil until the tomato pieces begin to break up. Season with the salt and pepper.

Toss together the little gem leaves and tomato dressing, scattering the torn basil leaves over the top.

more
Here are more than a few extras that can be added:
- *sliced red onion or spring onions*
- *mozzarella, feta or goat's cheese*
- *cucumber*
- *olives*
- *balsamic vinegar*
- *a trickle of crème fraîche*

serves four

250g (9oz) cherry tomatoes, quartered
4 tablespoons olive oil
sea salt and pepper
4 little gems
a handful of basil leaves, torn

cool cucumber slice

This must be one of the simplest recipes in the book. It's literally just a plate of sliced cucumber, but ice cold and with a good dressing and creamy touch, it is so refreshing.

Slice the cucumber thinly using a mandolin. Put the slices in a colander over a bowl and sprinkle with ¼ teaspoon table salt. Mix the salt into the slices and leave to stand for 20 minutes (the salt will draw out the excess water in the cucumber, leaving a fuller flavour and better texture).

After 20 minutes, taste a slice. If it is slightly too salty, simply rinse under cold water. Drain or squeeze the water out again.

Arrange the slices to cover two plates in an overlapping, carpaccio style or simply spoon into a rustic pile. Refrigerate to chill.

Whisk together the olive oil, white wine vinegar and 1 teaspoon of the lime juice. Season with salt and a twist of pepper. A splash or two of the remaining lime juice can be stirred into the crème fraîche.

To serve, drizzle the cucumber slices with the crème fraîche and vinaigrette.

more
- *Fresh chopped herbs can be added to the vinaigrette or sprigs of fresh herbs piled in the centre of the cucumber with a few green leaves to create a nice salad.*

serves two

1 large chilled cucumber, peeled
table salt, sea salt and pepper
2 tablespoons extra-virgin olive oil
1 teaspoon white wine vinegar
juice of 1 lime
2–3 tablespoons crème fraîche or sour cream

simple salad

Purely lettuce leaves and sprigs of fresh herbs. With it there's a choice of three dressings. If you want to impress, all can be offered, or choose just one for drizzling over. There's also a list of possible additions.

Tear any large round lettuce leaves and mix them in a large salad bowl with all the remaining ingredients.

serves six–eight

1 round lettuce, leaves separated
4 small little gems, leaves separated
1 iceberg, quartered and torn into pieces
1 bunch of chervil, picked into sprigs
½ bunch of flat-leaf parsley, picked
  into sprigs
a handful of tarragon leaves
1 bunch of chives, cut into 2cm
  (¾ inch) sticks

for the basic dressing
100ml (3½fl oz) olive oil / juice of ½ lemon / 1 tablespoon white wine vinegar / 1 tablespoon sherry vinegar (if unavailable, use white wine vinegar) / salt and pepper
Mix all the ingredients together and keep in an airtight jar.

for the citrus dressing
juice of 1 orange and finely grated zest of ½ orange / juice of 1 lemon and finely grated zest of ½ lemon / 1 tablespoon caster sugar / 1 teaspoon Dijon mustard (optional) / 6 tablespoons olive oil / salt and pepper
Place the orange and lemon zest in a small saucepan with the orange juice. Bring to a simmer and cook until just one third of the liquid is left. Remove from the heat and allow to cool. Whisk together the lemon juice, sugar and mustard, if using. Whisk the olive oil into the mixture and add the reduced orange juice and zests. Season with salt and pepper and the dressing is ready.

for the mozzarella, tomato, black olive, basil and garlic dressing
1 large clove of garlic, crushed / 50ml (2fl oz) olive oil / 1–2 tablespoons balsamic vinegar / 1 heaped tablespoon quartered and stoned black olives / 2 tomatoes, quartered, deseeded and chopped / 1 buffalo mozzarella, chopped / a handful of torn basil leaves
Whisk together the garlic, olive oil and balsamic vinegar, to taste. Add the remaining ingredients just before serving.

more
Some salad additions:
- *bread croutons or crostini / orange or grapefruit segments / red onion / toasted pine nuts or sesame seeds / melon or mango chunks / beetroot / lamb's lettuce, rocket or watercress*

mixed fennel, asparagus, grapefruit and apple

The fennel and asparagus are both best cut on a mandolin for extra thin and tender slices. Melon is also included in this recipe and Ogen, Charentais or watermelon all fit the bill. The dressing for this salad I've also used on page 42 to accompany the smoked trout. If you have walnut oil, it can be used here.

To make the dressing, stir together the vinegar and lemon juice in a small bowl, adding the two oils and whisking the vinaigrette slowly into the cream. Season with salt and pepper. The dressing can be stored in a screw-top jar or squeezy bottle in the refrigerator, keeping for up to 5 days (depending on the age of the cream).

Remove the outside layer from the fennel and shred it finely, preferably on a mandolin. Cut away the woody base to each asparagus and slice the spears thinly lengthways.

Top and tail the grapefruit, slicing down following the natural shape of the fruit and removing all skin and pith. Cut between each membrane to release the segments. Halve the segments. Quarter each apple and remove the core, cutting each piece into thin slices.

Mix all the vegetables and fruit together in a bowl with the melon, salad leaves and crostini, if using. Drizzle with the dressing and present in one large or four to six individual bowls. Offer any extra dressing separately.

more
- *A trickle of neat walnut or olive oil can be drizzled over the salad.*
- *This salad also works well with soft creamy goat's cheese. If you fancy cooking, breadcrumbed and deep-fried goat's cheese is even better.*

serves four–six

2 medium fennel bulbs or 4 baby fennel bulbs
8–10 asparagus spears
1 grapefruit
1 red apple
1 green apple
1 small or ½ medium melon, skinned, deseeded and chopped
1 bag of mixed salad leaves
15–20 crispy crostini (optional)

for the dressing
2 teaspoons white wine vinegar
2 tablespoons lemon juice
2 tablespoons groundnut or grape seed oil
6 tablespoons hazelnut or walnut oil
6 tablespoons double cream
sea salt and pepper

charcuterie board with celeriac, apple, pear and walnut coleslaw

Charcuterie literally means cooked meat and covers a whole range of salamis, hams and terrines. Parma, Bayonne and Serrano hams (Italian, French and Spanish) are probably the best known, not forgetting the Spanish Ibérico. There are also endless salamis to choose from, along with pâtés and terrines, all of which will go well with this home-made coleslaw.

Cut away the tough woody skin of the celeriac and slice on a mandolin into fine sticks. The apples and pears can also be cored and then cut into sticks on the mandolin, leaving the skin on, or cut or grated by hand.

Add the fruit to the celeriac along with the sliced celery, onion, if using, and walnuts. Stir in the lemon juice and season with salt and pepper.

Mix together 200g (7oz) of the mayonnaise with the Dijon mustard, spooning the sauce through the fruit and vegetables. For a looser dressing, add the remaining mayonnaise. Check for seasoning.

Arrange the chosen charcuterie on a board or platter with the coleslaw to serve.

more
- *Chopped flat-leaf parsley can be stirred into the coleslaw.*
- *For an extra nutty taste or as an alternative to the walnuts, add a tablespoon or two of toasted sesame seeds.*

serves six–eight

1 small or ½ large celeriac
2 apples
2 pears
4 sticks of celery, peeled and thinly sliced
1 small red onion, very thinly sliced (optional)
100g (4oz) walnuts, chopped
juice of 1 lemon
salt and pepper
200–300g (7–10oz) mayonnaise
1 teaspoon Dijon or wholegrain mustard
mixed charcuterie (about 200g/7oz per person for a light lunch or 300g/10oz for supper)

whipped stilton with figs and watercress

Crumble the Stilton into a small food processor and whip until softened, adding 125ml (4½fl oz) of the crème fraîche until a creamy consistency is reached. The remaining 25ml (1fl oz) of crème fraîche can also be whipped into the Stilton for a softer finish. The whipped Stilton can be eaten at room temperature or chilled for a firmer texture.

Put the redcurrant jelly, red wine vinegar and port, if using, in a small bowl and whisk until smooth. Stir in the oil and season with salt and pepper.

Present the whipped Stilton either scrolled as you would ice cream, or simply dolloped onto plates. Arrange the figs alongside the Stilton, topped with sprigs of watercress and chopped walnuts, if using. Drizzle with the redcurrant dressing and sprinkle with a little sea salt and twist of pepper.

more
- *Slices of walnut, raisin or granary bread all accompany the whipped Stilton and figs very well.*

serves four

225g (8oz) Stilton
125–150ml (4½–5½fl oz)
    crème fraîche, to loosen
6 figs, quartered
1 bunch of watercress,
    washed and torn into sprigs
1 heaped tablespoon
    chopped walnuts (optional)
sea salt and pepper

for the dressing
1 tablespoon redcurrant jelly
1 tablespoon red wine
    vinegar
1 tablespoon port (this can
    be replaced with vinegar)
4 tablespoons walnut or olive
    oil
sea salt and pepper

quick fixes –
fast food in 15 minutes

quick fixes –
fast food in 15 minutes

Well, there'll certainly be no stews, rice or potato dishes in this chapter. If fifteen minutes is what you've got, then the punchy flavour of your ingredients is always going to be your most important asset. The excitement for me of thinking of recipes to cook in such a short time is that it pares my ideas back down to the essentials. Flavour comes to the forefront and fussy details are dispensed with. Simplicity is key.

As you would expect, there are a couple of pastas here (prawns, pancetta, pasta and lemon and parmesan pasta), but I've also included a t-bone steak with melting roquefort cherry tomatoes and bittersweet beef fillet leaves to show you that, if you concentrate on cooking one element well and keeping the garnishes simple, a complete meal in under fifteen minutes is well within anyone's grasp.

Again, your secret weapon is the seasonal ingredient. When British asparagus is in season in May, the only question can be why cook anything else? And the beauty of it is that, like all prime ingredients, they taste at their best cooked simply. Grilling with a little ham and cheese is a dinner I would gladly toil far longer than fifteen minutes over.

The under fifteen minutes tag does put these recipes firmly in the after work suppers or even lunches category. I can't think of anything more uplifting than opening up a lunchbox of smoked salmon and fennel salad or warm salmon on brown bread with cucumber mayonnaise. If you're making dinner for friends, one of these recipes chosen as a starter (the beetroot carpaccio with redcurrant walnut dressing is a perfect example) would certainly take the time pressure off.

chilled melon and basil soup

A very refreshing start to any meal, particularly during the hottest months of the year. For maximum flavour, it's important that the fruits are ripe.

Peel the mangoes and cut away all of the flesh from the stones.

Cut the melon into six wedges, removing the seeds and cutting away the skin. Place all the fruit in a blender, in batches if necessary, with the ice cubes and blend to a purée.

Stir in the basil and divide the soup into four bowls or cups. The soup is ready to serve or finish with a few sea salt crystals, a twist of pepper and a trickle of walnut oil, if using.

serves four as a starter

2 mangoes
1 large Charentais melon
4–6 ice cubes
8 basil leaves, chopped
sea salt and pepper
   (optional)
a trickle of walnut oil
   (optional)

courgette soup with tomato and red onion bruschetta

Boil some water in a kettle. Put the chopped courgettes into a saucepan and pour 600ml (1 pint) boiling water on top. Bring to the boil and cook for 6 to 7 minutes until the courgettes are tender. Season with salt and pepper and liquidize until smooth in a blender.

Meanwhile, rub the cut side of the garlic halves over the toasted bread on each side. Mix together the tomato, sliced onion and basil with a drop or two of olive oil. Season with salt and pepper and arrange the topping on the four toasts.

Place the toasts in four soup plates or bowls (or offer separately) and pour the hot soup around them.

more
- *One vegetable stock cube can be crumbled over the courgettes before adding the boiling water, if preferred.*
- *A buffalo mozzarella can be divided into four slices and lightly melted on top of each garlic toast before spooning on the tomato, onion and basil.*

serves four

450g (1lb) courgettes, roughly chopped into small pieces
salt and pepper

for the bruschettas
1 clove of garlic, peeled and halved
4 thick slices of French bread or ciabatta, toasted
2 plum tomatoes, deseeded and cut into thin strips
1 small red onion, thinly sliced
4 basil leaves, shredded
olive oil
sea salt and pepper

hot asparagus spears glazed with ham, cheddar and parmesan

Preheat the grill.

Snap away the woody end of each asparagus spear.

Place the spears in a deep saucepan on top of the stove, boil a kettle of water and pour it over them, adding a pinch of salt. Reheat until boiling again and cook for 2 to 3 minutes until just tender. Drain, adding the knob of butter and seasoning with salt and pepper.

Put half the spears in an earthenware dish and top with two slices of ham, leaving the asparagus tops exposed. Mix the two cheeses together and scatter half over the ham. Place under the grill until just beginning to melt. Top with the remaining spears, ham and cheese and return under the grill until melted with a light golden finish.

serves four

2 bunches of asparagus
(8–10 spears per person)
salt and pepper
a large knob of butter
4 slices of ham
100g (4oz) Cheddar cheese, grated
100g (4oz) Parmesan cheese, grated

fiery mushrooms on toast

To achieve this recipe in under 15 minutes simply requires quick chopping and slicing before taking on the heat of the grill. This is delicious to eat as a quick lunch or supper dish, almost becoming a full meal when accompanied by a tossed green salad.

Preheat the grill.

Mix together the chopped garlic, chilli and red onion, if using, stirring in half the olive oil to loosen.

Place the mushrooms flat-side down on a greased baking tray. Spoon the garlic chilli mix over each one, seasoning with a sprinkling of sea salt. Grill the mushrooms not too close to the heat for 10 to 12 minutes until tender.

Meanwhile, toast the French bread slices on both sides and keep warm to one side.

Spoon the mushrooms on to the bread slices, sprinkling liberally with the chopped parsley.

Mix together the remaining olive oil, red wine vinegar and any cooking juices and drizzle generously over each portion.

serves four

2 cloves of garlic, chopped
2 fresh red chillies, thinly sliced
½ small red onion or 1 shallot, very thinly sliced (optional)
4 tablespoons olive oil
8 large Portobello mushrooms
sea salt
4 thick slices of French bread
a handful of picked curly parsley, roughly chopped
1 tablespoon red wine vinegar

beetroot carpaccio with redcurrant walnut dressing

This recipe I've kept very simple by using precooked beetroots. Should you wish to cook your own, the recipe will become one to fit in the cooking for pleasure category. As mentioned, this is a basic recipe, but broken nuggets of goat's cheese and walnuts can be added to the salad leaves, perhaps along with chopped chives for an oniony taste.

Slice the beetroots thinly on a mandolin and arrange on four medium-sized plates, slightly overlapping them to cover the plates. Season with salt and pepper.

Gently warm together the redcurrant jelly and red wine vinegar, allowing the jelly to melt. Once melted, remove from the heat and whisk in the Dijon mustard followed by the walnut or hazelnut oil. Season with salt and pepper.

Drizzle or brush the dressing over the beetroot and arrange a small pile of the salad leaves in the centre of each plate.

serves four

6 medium/large cooked and
    peeled beetroots
sea salt and pepper
a handful or two of rocket
    and watercress or mixed
    salad leaves

for the dressing
1 level tablespoon
    redcurrant jelly
2 tablespoons red wine
    vinegar (preferably
    Cabernet Sauvignon)
1 level teaspoon Dijon
    mustard
4 tablespoons walnut or
    hazelnut oil
salt and pepper

smoked salmon and fennel salad

Salad leaves of your choice can be added to this recipe, along with a few very thin slices of red onion for an extra tang.

Using a mandolin, shred the fennel into paper thin slices.

Whisk together the wholegrain mustard, honey, lemon juice and olive oil, seasoning with salt and a twist of pepper.

Add the fennel to the dressing and begin to divide among the plates, tearing the smoked salmon slices into strips and adding as you arrange the salads.

more
* A few picked sprigs of dill can be used should the fennel be without its herby top.

serves four

2 fennel bulbs, trimmed
   (saving any fennel top
   feathery sprigs)
1 tablespoon wholegrain
   mustard
2 tablespoons honey
2 tablespoons lemon juice
2 tablespoons olive oil
salt and pepper
200g (7oz) sliced smoked
   salmon

grilled red radicchio with snapped parma ham and sour cream

Preheat the grill.

Trim the radicchio of any damaged leaves before splitting each in half or, if large, into quarters. Quickly rinse, shake off any excess water and place on a baking tray. Season with salt and pepper and drizzle the eight radicchio halves with four tablespoons of the olive oil.

Divide the butter among the halves and place the radicchio beneath the grill, not too close to the top, for 8 to 10 minutes.

Meanwhile, heat the remaining olive oil in a frying pan over a medium heat. Put the Parma ham slices in the pan and fry for a few minutes on both sides until they have become crisp like crackling.

Arrange the grilled radicchio on plates, drizzling with any juices left on the tray. Snap the Parma ham rashers and place on top, offering the sour cream to spoon over.

more
- *Some chunky nuggets of Gorgonzola and even a few broken walnuts can be scattered over the radicchio before grilling.*

serves four

4 small red radicchio heads
sea salt and pepper
6 tablespoons olive oil
25g (1oz) butter
4 slices of Parma ham
4 heaped tablespoons sour
   cream

broken feta cheese salad with apples and pears

Mix together the salad and chicory leaves in a bowl. Core and slice the apple and pear and add to the salad with the chopped walnuts and feta.

Whisk together the vinegar, sugar and oils, seasoning with salt and a twist of pepper. Spoon the dressing over the salad, gently mixing it all together before dividing among the plates.

more
- *Add a squeeze of lemon or lime to the dressing.*
- *A few sprigs of chervil, parsley or chive sticks can be added to the salad.*

serves two for supper or
   four as a starter

1 bag of mixed salad leaves
1 chicory head, trimmed and
   divided into leaves
1 apple
1 pear
a handful of roughly
   chopped walnuts
225g (8oz) feta cheese,
   broken into pieces
2 tablespoons cider vinegar
pinch of caster sugar
2 tablespoons walnut oil
2 tablespoons groundnut oil,
   plus extra for brushing
sea salt and pepper

warm salmon on brown bread with cucumber mayonnaise

The salmon takes less than 10 minutes to cook and during that time, the rest of the sandwich is prepared. A thick slice of smoked salmon would also work very well with the cucumber, the sandwich taking just a few minutes in total to make. The cucumber can be peeled or the skin left on.

Heat a non-stick frying pan with the butter or oil. Once sizzling, season the salmon with salt and pepper and place, skinned-side down, in the pan. Lightly fry for 3 to 4 or 5 minutes, depending on thickness of the slices, before turning the fillets over and removing the pan from the stove. The residual heat in the pan will continue to cook the fish for a further few minutes.

Meanwhile, slice the cucumber and put in a bowl. Add a squeeze of lime juice and the sugar, if using, stir it all together and season with salt and pepper.

Spread the bread liberally with the mayonnaise before adding the cucumber (a small dollop of mayonnaise can also be spooned on top of the cucumber). Place the salmon on the cucumber and the open sandwich is complete.

more
• *Chopped dill can be added to the cucumber.*

serves two

a large knob of butter or 1 tablespoon olive oil
2 x 100g (4oz) slices of salmon fillet (175g/6oz for a full meal), skinned
salt and pepper
½ small cucumber (see left)
a squeeze of lime juice (optional)
a pinch of sugar (optional)
2 thick slices of brown or granary bread
mayonnaise, for spreading

lemon and parmesan pasta

Cook the pasta in boiling salted water until tender but leaving a slight bite.

Meanwhile, finely grate 1 heaped teaspoon lemon zest before halving and juicing the lemon.

Warm together the lemon zest, lemon juice and 1 to 2 tablespoons water. Once simmering, whisk in 50g (2oz) of the butter until completely combined. For a richer sauce, stir in the remaining 25g (1oz) and cook for 2 to 3 minutes.

Once the pasta is cooked, drain and season with a pinch of salt and a generous twist of black pepper. Stir in a trickle of olive oil, along with the lemon butter and half of the grated Parmesan.

Divide the pasta among four bowls, drizzling each with a little more olive oil and offering the extra Parmesan for sprinkling.

more
- *Shredded and buttered spring onions and sliced button mushrooms are good additions.*

serves four

400–500g (14–18oz) dried pasta
1 lemon
50–75g (2–3oz) butter, chopped
salt and pepper
olive oil, for drizzling
50–100g (2–4oz) Parmesan cheese, finely grated (or any cheese you happen to have)

pan-fried white fish with buttery grapes and chervil

There are endless white fish to choose from: Dover sole, lemon sole, plaice, halibut, hake, John Dory, cod and turbot will all suit the flavours of the grapes and chervil. As for time, even the thickest fillet of halibut or cod will cook in just two thirds of our 15 minutes. Baby leaf spinach can be served along with this dish and is to be found picked and washed in most supermarkets.

Heat a frying pan with the olive oil. Once hot, season the fish with salt and pepper and place it in the pan, skinned-side down. Fry over a medium heat for 5 to 6 minutes until golden brown. Add a knob of butter and, once sizzling, turn the fish, basting with the butter. Remove from the heat, leaving the fish in the pan for a further 1 to 2 minutes before serving.

Meanwhile, warm a frying pan or saucepan with the remaining knob of butter. Add the grapes and gently fry until they begin to soften. Season with salt and pepper, adding a squeeze of lemon juice and 2 tablespoons water. Stir in 50g (2oz) of the chilled butter, not allowing it to boil but just to barely simmer. For a richer taste, add the remaining butter before stirring in the chopped chervil.

Present the turbot on a plate, spooning over the buttery grapes and chervil.

serves four

olive oil
4 x 150–175g (5–6oz) turbot
    fillets (or other white fish),
    skinned
salt and pepper
2 knobs of butter
300g (10oz) seedless white
    grapes, halved
a squeeze of lemon juice
50–75g (2–3oz) cold butter,
    diced
2 tablespoons finely
    chopped chervil

bittersweet beef fillet leaves

The leaves are salad leaves, either one variety or a selection – the choice is yours. This recipe is suitable as a supper dish for two, while one extra fillet would be more than enough for four starters.

Heat a frying pan with the vegetable oil. Once smoking, season the beef fillets with salt and pepper. Put the two steaks in the pan and fry over a high heat for a few minutes, allowing them to colour until almost burnt before turning and repeating. A few minutes on each side will leave a medium-rare finish. The burnt tinges provide the bitter flavour. Remove the steaks and set aside to rest.

Slightly reduce the heat and add the honey. Once bubbling, remove the pan from the heat and pour in the red wine vinegar and oil. Season with salt and pepper.

Meanwhile, divide the salad leaves between two plates. Cut directly through the steaks, forming rectangular-shaped slices. Scatter the steak slices over the salad, drizzling each with the dressing.

more
- *Crispy crostini toasts (available ready-made) and chunks of blue cheese or Brie make tasty additions.*

serves two

1 tablespoon vegetable oil
2 x 100g (4oz) beef fillet
  steaks
salt and pepper
1 teaspoon honey
2 teaspoons red wine vinegar
2 tablespoons olive or walnut
  oil
2 generous handfuls of salad
  leaves, rinsed

prawns, pancetta, pasta

Cook the pasta in boiling salted water following the packet cooking time (usually 5 to 7 minutes) until tender but leaving a slight bite, then drain.

Meanwhile, heat a large deep frying pan or wok. Once hot, fry the pancetta for a few minutes until golden brown. Add the garlic and butter, stirring for a further minute over a medium heat.

Scatter in the prawns and a trickle of olive oil and stir for a further minute or 2 before adding the cooked pasta. Toss all together well, seasoning with just a pinch of salt and a good twist of pepper. Sprinkle with the chopped parsley and serve.

more
One or two extras can be added:
- *a few dollops of crème fraîche stirred in for a creamy touch*
- *shavings or grated Parmesan cheese*
- *a large wedge of lemon on the side*

serves four

400g (14oz) 'quick cook' pasta (penne, spiralli or spaghetti)
225g (8oz) pancetta cubes
2 cloves of garlic, chopped
25g (1oz) butter
350g (12oz) ready to eat peeled prawns
extra-virgin olive oil, for cooking
sea salt and pepper
1 heaped tablespoon roughly chopped parsley

t-bone steak with melting roquefort cherry tomatoes

A T-bone steak comprises the sirloin and fillet steaks, connected together by the T-shaped bone. The steaks are of various thicknesses and weights and what you choose really depends on how much you fancy eating. I'd suggest buying a steak weighing between 450–600g (1lb–1lb 5oz) to really appreciate the full texture. The steaks can be pan-fried or cooked in a grill pan.

Preheat a frying pan or grill pan and the grill.

Season the steaks with salt and pepper, drizzling over a tablespoon of the olive oil between the two.

The steaks can now be placed in the preheated pan and cooked for 3 to 4 minutes on each side until medium rare to medium.

Meanwhile, fry the shallots in the remaining olive oil for a few minutes until they begin to soften. Add the cherry tomatoes and continue to fry over a high heat until the cherry tomatoes are softening. Season with salt and pepper.

Top the steaks with the tomatoes and Roquefort and place under the grill, allowing the cheese to soften and melt.

Arrange the steaks on plates, drizzling any juices over the top and finishing with a dollop of crème fraîche, if using.

more
• A simple watercress salad dressed with a little balsamic and olive oil will more than complete this dish.

serves two

2 x T-bone steaks (see left)
salt and pepper
4 tablespoons olive oil
2 tablespoons finely
  chopped shallots
225g (8oz) punnet of cherry
  tomatoes, halved
100g (4oz) Roquefort cheese,
  crumbled into small pieces
2 tablespoons crème fraîche
  (optional)

ready in 20 to 30 minutes

ready in 20 to 30 minutes

Cooking a fabulous meal in under half an hour is not without its challenges. If you're thinking meat, then it must be a piece that can be swiftly grilled or pan-fried. This means looking for the tenderest (and often most expensive) cuts. An alternative is to follow in the footsteps of many Asian cooks and speed up the cooking process by frying small pieces of meat over a very high heat. This is the method I've used most successfully for my stir-fried chicken with tomatoes, basil and crispy parmesan and the lemon and chilli sesame pork with mangetout.

I've also included lots of fish and seafood in this chapter because, so quick to cook, they invariably produce an impressive meal. Of course, your fish must be very fresh, so if you are someone who usually picks up a few ingredients on your way home from work, then these recipes are perfect for you. Simply stop off at the fishmonger for a piece of salmon and tip some pine nuts, a lemon, French beans and perhaps a bottle of white wine into your shopping basket at the supermarket and a piece of salmon with roasted pine nut and lemon french beans is just thirty minutes (plus perhaps a bus or train ride home) away.

Fish is also fantastic if you're having friends for dinner because it is somehow always a bit special, yet is best prepared quickly and with little fuss. If I was entertaining friends on a Friday after work, pan-fried sea bass with smoked bacon and caper cabbage or the seared halibut with a blood orange and basil courgette salad would be perfect.

This chapter is also one where pasta (10 to 15 minutes cooking time) and potatoes (20 minutes) are going to be your staple accompaniments. The classic risotto milanese just squeezes into a half hour, although the pace of cooking in fact seems quite leisurely. And if you think cooking in under half an hour has to mean basic food, the regal roast chateaubriand with macaroni cheese will show you that you can still eat the very best, cooking food in the time it takes to order a pizza.

savoury pear, stilton and chive cakes with a red wine honey dressing

These 'cakes' are simply a variation on Scotch pancakes and would work well as a savoury dessert alternative or as a supper dish.

Sift the flour and salt into a bowl. Whisk in the eggs and milk to make a smooth batter, then stir in the chives.

If you're using rings, grease six 7–8cm (2½–3 inch) diameter rings (the kind used for frying eggs or making small tartlets) liberally with butter. Heat a non-stick frying pan with a trickle of olive oil and place the rings in the pan. Divide half the batter among the rings and cook over a medium heat for 3 to 4 minutes until bubbles appear and the cakes are beginning to set around the edges. Lift the rings from the cakes and, using a spatula, turn them over in the pan, cooking for a further 2 to 3 minutes until they are a light golden brown. These can now be kept warm, while you cook the remaining batter in the rings.

Meanwhile, remove the central core from each pear quarter and heat a second frying pan with a trickle of olive oil and the butter. Once it begins to sizzle, add the pear and cook over a medium heat, turning from time to time, for 6 to 7 minutes until just tender. Preheat the grill.

Put the cakes on a baking tray, topping each one with a pear quarter and the crumbled Stilton. Finish the cakes under the grill, placing them not too close to the heat, but just allowing the cheese to soften and melt.

Arrange the cakes on six plates. Whisk together the walnut or olive oil, red wine vinegar and honey. Season with salt and a twist of pepper and drizzle over the cakes. Scatter with a few salad leaves to garnish, if using.

serves six

225g (8oz) self-raising flour
½ teaspoon salt
2 eggs
200ml (7fl oz) milk
1 bunch of chives, finely chopped
olive oil, for cooking
3 pears, quartered
25g (1oz) butter
225g (8oz) Stilton cheese, crumbled into chunks
chard, rocket or mixed leaves (optional)

for the dressing
4 tablespoons walnut or olive oil
2 tablespoons red wine vinegar
2 teaspoons honey
sea salt and pepper

a bowl of cauliflower and camembert

Chunks of crusty bread for dunking in the soup and picking up melting Camembert complete this dish.

Put the cauliflower florets, milk, stock cube and Dijon mustard in a saucepan with 500ml (18fl oz) water. Bring to a simmer and cook for 20 minutes until the cauliflower is tender and completely cooked through.

Season the soup with salt and pepper and liquidize in a blender until smooth.

Rewarm the soup with the cream, if using, and divide among the bowls. Finish with chunks of Camembert, a drizzle of olive oil and a sprinkling of freshly grated nutmeg, if using.

more
- *Brie or a soft Gorgonzola are tasty alternatives to Camembert.*
- *Some of the small cauliflower florets can be cooked separately until just tender, using them to garnish the soup.*

serves four

1 large cauliflower or 2 small–medium, trimmed and divided into florets
500ml (18fl oz) milk
½ vegetable stock cube (optional) (see note on page 8)
1 teaspoon Dijon mustard
salt and pepper
100–150ml (3½–5fl oz) single cream (optional)
225g (8oz) Camembert, broken into pieces
olive oil, for drizzling
freshly grated nutmeg (optional)

crispy lemon and parsley camembert with mango and spinach

It's important the Camembert wedges are cooked direct from the refrigerator. This will prevent the cheese from over melting as it fries. Although deep-fried in this recipe, the cheese wedges can be quickly pan-fried on each side in just a few millimetres of oil.

Finely grate the zest from the lemon and stir it into the breadcrumbs with the chopped parsley, seasoning with salt and pepper.

Whisk the egg in a bowl with a splash of milk to loosen it. Lightly flour each of the Camembert wedges before dipping in the egg and rolling in the breadcrumbs to coat. Refrigerate once all are well covered with the crumbs.

Heat a few inches of oil in a large frying pan, wok or deep-fat fryer to 180°C (350°F). Once hot, deep-fry the Camembert for a few minutes or more until golden brown. Carefully remove using a slotted spoon and drain on kitchen paper.

Meanwhile, mix together the mango, spinach and spring onion, if using, and season with a pinch of sea salt and a twist of pepper.

Present the crispy Camembert with the mango and spinach, finishing with a squeeze of lemon juice and a drizzle of olive oil.

more

• *Once the oil for deep-frying reaches 180°C (350°F) it's important to maintain the temperature over a low heat to prevent the oil from becoming too hot.*

serves four–six

1 lemon
4 thick slices of white
   bread, crusts removed
   and crumbled or 6
   heaped tablespoons dried
   breadcrumbs
a handful of picked curly
   parsley, chopped
sea salt and pepper
1 egg
a splash of milk
1 chilled Camembert, cut
   into 6–8 wedges
flour, for dusting
sunflower oil, for frying
1 mango, peeled and
   chopped or sliced
2 handfuls (approximately
   150g/5oz) of washed baby
   spinach leaves
2–3 spring onions, finely
   shredded (optional)
extra-virgin olive oil, to drizzle

mushroom and goat's cheese tartlets

These have been kept very basic and simple with just four main ingredients: the pastry, mushrooms, red onion and goat's cheese. There are then only a few extras with the sherry vinegar and walnut dressing plus the salad leaves. These are not essential, but do add extra flavour to the finished dish. Shavings of Parmesan cheese strewn across the top would be another flavoursome addition.

Preheat the oven to 200°C/400°F/gas 6.

In a frying pan, quickly fry the sliced onion in the butter until beginning to soften, seasoning with salt and pepper.

Cut the pastry into four approximately 11cm (4½ inch) squares. Any excess pastry can be frozen for later use.

Remove the stalks from the mushrooms and season with salt and pepper, placing them cup-side up on the pastry squares.

Spoon the onion on top of the mushrooms and bake in the oven for 15 minutes before placing the goat's cheese slices on top. Season with a twist of pepper and sprinkling of sea salt and continue to bake for a further 5 minutes until the cheese is beginning to soften.

While baking the tartlets, whisk together the sherry vinegar, walnut and groundnut oil and season with salt and pepper.

To serve, arrange a few salad leaves on top of each tartlet, sprinkling with the dressing, or offer the salad leaves apart.

more
- *For extra colour, the tartlets can be finished off beneath the grill.*

serves four

2 red onions, sliced
a knob of butter
sea salt and pepper
1 sheet of ready-rolled puff pastry
4 large flat mushrooms
4 thick slices (about 50–60g/2–2½oz each) of goat's cheese loaf
1½ tablespoons sherry vinegar
2 tablespoons walnut oil
1 tablespoon groundnut oil
a handful or two of mixed salad leaves

linguine and pesto frittata with asparagus, spinach, peas

A large ovenproof frying pan is needed for this recipe

Preheat the oven to 190°C/375°F/gas 5.

Cook the linguine in boiling salted water following the packet cooking time, before draining.

Meanwhile, heat the ovenproof frying pan with a tablespoon or two of olive oil. Add the sliced onion, gently frying for 6 to 7 minutes until beginning to soften.

While frying the onion, cut the asparagus into 5cm (2 inch) pieces, discarding the woody base of each spear. These can now be cooked in boiling salted water for just 2 to 3 minutes until tender. Drain once cooked, tipping them into a large bowl and mixing with the spinach leaves and peas.

Pour the cream and beaten eggs over the asparagus, spinach and peas and stir in the pesto, onion and drained linguine. Mix together well, adding the Parmesan cheese, if using, and seasoning with salt and pepper.

Rewarm the frying pan with 2 tablespoons of the olive oil and carefully pour the linguine mixture into the pan. Shake the pan to spread the pasta and vegetables evenly, frying over a medium heat for 2 to 3 minutes to set the base. The frittata can now be finished off in the preheated oven for a further 20 to 25 minutes or until set.

Once cooked, olive oil can be drizzled over the top before serving.

more

- *Slices or chopped mozzarella can be scattered over the top during the frittata's last few minutes in the oven, softening and melting before serving.*
- *Sprigs of chervil, flat-leaf parsley and basil leaves sprinkled over at the end offer another 'green' flavour. Rocket leaves are also an attractive and tasty supplement.*

serves four–six

225g (8oz) linguine (or spaghetti or tagliatelle)
olive oil, for cooking and drizzling
1 onion, sliced
1 bunch of asparagus (about 12 spears)
100g (4oz) washed baby spinach leaves (approximately ½ bag)
100g (4oz) frozen peas, defrosted
150ml (5fl oz) double cream
6 large eggs, beaten
2 heaped tablespoons pesto
4 heaped tablespoons freshly grated Parmesan cheese (optional)
salt and pepper

sesame wild mushroom salad

Wild mushrooms are in season during the autumn and winter months, with one or two varieties showing their face during the spring and summer. They can be purchased as individual varieties or in mixed packs. Chestnut mushrooms would also be a good addition to this salad, adding another nutty flavour.

Chop or tear any large wild mushrooms into bite-sized pieces.

Whisk together the vinaigrette ingredients and season with salt and pepper.

Fry the sesame seeds in a dry pan until toasted and golden brown, then remove from the pan to prevent further cooking.

Reheat the frying pan and once very hot, scatter in the mushrooms and sesame oil and season with salt and pepper. Stir and fry for a minute or two, leaving texture in the mushrooms.

Meanwhile, cut away the stalks and any yellow leaves from the watercress and discard, then toss together the watercress and spinach in a bowl. Add the toasted sesame seeds to the mushrooms and spoon over the leaves with the vinaigrette. Stir until the leaves begin to wilt before sharing the salad among four plates or bowls.

more
- *Cubes of Fontina or goat's cheese can be added to the mushrooms once fried and the cheese allowed to slightly soften.*
- *A splash of soy or Worcester sauce can be added to the vinaigrette for a tangy taste.*

serves four

350g (12oz) mixed or one variety of wild mushrooms, rinsed
2 teaspoons sesame seeds
2 tablespoons sesame oil
sea salt and pepper
100g (4oz) bag of washed watercress
200g (8oz) bag of washed baby spinach leaves

for the vinaigrette
1 tablespoon sesame oil
1 tablespoon groundnut oil
2 teaspoons sherry vinegar
1 tablespoon honey
salt and pepper

tiger prawns and tomatoes with basil and garlic mayonnaise

Peel the tiger prawns, leaving the tails intact. To devein, cut down the back of the prawns using a sharp knife and remove the thin digestive tract. If you want to butterfly them, simply cut slightly deeper to open up the backs.

Spoon the mayonnaise, herbs and garlic into a small food processor and whiz until completely mixed together, finishing with a squeeze of lemon juice and twist of pepper. If mixing by hand, finely chop the garlic before adding.

With the point of a knife, remove the eye from the tomatoes. Cut a cross in each base and blanch in a bowl of boiling water for 10 seconds before plunging into iced water. Once cold, the skin peels away easily. Peel, halve and deseed before cutting into cubes.

In a small bowl, pour just enough olive oil into the cubed tomato to loosen and add a dash of balsamic to sweeten and sharpen. Season with salt and pepper.

Heat a frying pan or grill pan with a trickle of olive oil and knob of butter. Once sizzling, add the prawns, cooking for just 1 to 2 minutes on each side until they turn pink. Season with salt and pepper.

Arrange the prawns on a warm plate, spooning over the tomato dressing. Serve the basil and garlic mayonnaise in a small bowl ready for dipping.

more
• A teaspoon of the herbs for the mayonnaise can be saved and added to the tomatoes. Alternatively, scatter over a few torn tarragon leaves.

serves two–four

12 large raw tiger prawns
100g (4oz) mayonnaise
2 tablespoons chopped basil
2 tablespoons chopped flat-leaf parsley
2 cloves of garlic, chopped
a squeeze of lemon juice
sea salt and pepper
2 plum tomatoes
extra-virgin olive oil, to loosen
a dash of balsamic vinegar
olive oil, for cooking
a knob of butter

quick curried prawns

This dish can be eaten as a main course with plain rice or served just warm with torn or shredded iceberg leaves for an alternative prawn cocktail.

Twist the heads from the tiger prawns and peel, leaving the tails intact and retaining all the shells. To devein, cut down the back of the prawns using a sharp knife and remove the thin digestive tract.

To make the sauce, melt the knob of butter and add the prawn heads and shells, gently frying for 5 to 6 minutes. Pour in the brandy and cook until the liquid is almost dry before adding the curry powder, chicken stock and cream. Simmer rapidly until just two thirds of the liquid is left and it has reached a sauce consistency. Strain through a fine sieve, squeezing out any juice from the shells. Season the sauce with salt and pepper, finishing with a squeeze of lime.

To cook the prawns, heat a frying pan with a drop or two of the vegetable oil. Add the butter and once it begins to sizzle, fry the prawns for just a couple of minutes before turning and frying for a further 2 minutes until pink. Season with salt and pepper and stir in the curry sauce. The prawns are ready to serve.

more
- *A teaspoon or two of mango chutney can be added to the sauce with the stock and cream for a sweeter curry taste.*

serves two as a main or
three–four as a starter

12 large raw tiger prawns,
   shell on
vegetable oil, for cooking
a large knob of butter
salt and pepper

for the sauce
a knob of butter
2 tablespoons brandy
1 teaspoon curry powder
150ml (5fl oz) chicken stock
   (see note on page 8)
200ml (7fl oz) double cream
salt and pepper
a squeeze of lime

seared scallops and chilli-spiced cucumber

Slice the cucumber thinly on a mandolin into spaghetti-style or tagliatelle strips, discarding the central seed core.

Add the chopped chilli to the oil. Quickly warm together the soy sauce, sugar and vinegar and once the sugar has dissolved, whisk into the chilli oil, seasoning with a pinch of salt and a twist of pepper.

Scoop the cucumber into a bowl and stir in the dressing, checking for seasoning.

Halve each of the scallops to make two discs. Heat a frying pan with a drizzle of olive oil and once very hot, put the scallops in the pan and cook for just a minute or two before quickly turning and immediately removing. Season each with one or two sea salt crystals.

Divide the cucumber strips among four plates or bowls, drizzling with any remaining dressing before finishing with the seared scallop slices.

serves four as a starter

1 large cucumber, peeled
1 large fresh red chilli, halved, deseeded and finely chopped
3 tablespoons groundnut or grape seed oil
2 teaspoons soy sauce
1 teaspoon caster sugar
1 teaspoon white wine vinegar
sea salt and pepper
12 scallops, out of shell
olive oil, for cooking

more
- *Finely chopped chives or tarragon can be added to the 'spaghetti' or very thin, round slices of spring onion.*
- *A small dollop of crème fraîche, sour cream or natural yoghurt can be spooned on to each pile of cucumber before topping with the scallop slices.*
- *Lime can be squeezed over the top of the scallops.*

grilled mackerel with apples and onions

I'm adding cream to the apples here, but it's not essential. I've also kept the dish alcohol free, but a splash of Calvados is more than welcome. These are sort of starter portions with just one fillet of mackerel per person, however you can simply double the whole recipe for a main course.

Take your mackerel fillets and if the fine bones haven't been removed, simply pull them out with tweezers.

Heat a frying pan with a knob of butter. Once sizzling, add the sliced onion and pinch of sugar. Cook over a medium heat for 8 to 10 minutes until golden brown.

Add the chopped apple and continue to fry for a few minutes before pouring in 100ml (3½fl oz) of the apple juice. Increase the heat, allowing the juice to evaporate until almost dry. For a stronger apple taste, add the remaining juice and also reduce until almost dry. Pour in 100ml (3½fl oz) of the cream, bring to a simmer and season with salt and pepper. For a looser consistency, add the remaining cream.

Meanwhile, preheat the grill and lightly butter a baking tray, sprinkling with salt and pepper. Score the skin side of the mackerel fillets with a sharp knife and place them on the baking tray. Brush each fillet with the remaining knob of butter and season with salt and pepper. Cook under the grill for 4 to 5 minutes until golden brown.

Spoon the creamy apples and onions on to plates and top with the grilled mackerel.

more
- *A tablespoon of lightly chopped chervil can be added to the apple and onions.*

serves four as a starter

4 mackerel fillets
2 large knobs of butter
2 large onions, sliced
a pinch of sugar
2 apples, peeled, cored and chopped
100–150ml (3½–5fl oz) apple juice
100–150ml (3½–5fl oz) crème fraîche or double cream (optional)
sea salt and pepper

smoked haddock, poached egg, wilted rocket and sorrel hollandaise

There's just one addition to that ingredients list: watercress. Warmed and wilted with the rocket leaves, it gives a coarser texture and stronger pepper taste. It's important here that the sauce is made first and kept warm while poaching the smoked haddock and eggs.

To make the hollandaise, melt the butter in a small saucepan or place in a bowl, cover with clingfilm and microwave. Place the egg yolks and lemon juice in a blender and, while at maximum speed, slowly add the melted butter, continuing to blend until thick and creamy. Season with salt and cayenne pepper, stirring in an extra squeeze of lemon to finish it off. Keep warm to one side.

Bring the milk and 300ml (10fl oz) water to boil in a pan large enough to hold the haddock. Also fill a large saucepan with water and bring to a rapid simmer, ready for poaching the eggs.

Put the haddock in the milk and gently simmer for 3 to 4 minutes until just firm to the touch. Meanwhile, whisk the water in a circular motion in the saucepan, cracking and dropping the eggs into the centre one by one. The eggs will also take just 3 to 4 minutes to cook.

Rinse the watercress, shaking off the excess water and cutting away the main stalks. Heat a frying pan or wok with the knob of butter. Once bubbling, add the rocket leaves and sprigs of watercress, seasoning with salt and pepper. The leaves will just take a moment or two before wilting in the pan, ready to serve. Divide among four plates.

Using a fish slice, carefully lift the haddock from the milk, peeling away the skin if left on, before arranging on the plates with the poached eggs. Stir the sorrel into the hollandaise to finish the sauce and spoon over the top.

serves four

300ml (10fl oz) milk
4 x 100–175g (4–6oz) smoked haddock fillets (100g for a starter and 175g for a main course)
4 eggs
1 bunch of watercress
a knob of butter
100g (4oz) rocket
salt and pepper

for the sorrel hollandaise
175g (6oz) butter
3 egg yolks
juice of 1 lemon
salt
a pinch of cayenne or ground white pepper
10–12 sorrel leaves, shredded or chopped

pan-fried hake with ham, peas, broad beans and asparagus

This recipe may look daunting, but it's all quite easy. The hake is bought prepared, the ham is simply microwaved before breaking it up, the peas can be frozen and the broad beans and asparagus take just a few minutes. Incidentally, cod, halibut or turbot are good replacements for the hake.

Put the sliced shallots in a saucepan and top with the white wine. Bring to a rapid simmer and allow to reduce by three quarters. Add the bay leaf and chicken stock and continue to simmer gently.

Meanwhile, blanch the peas for 4 to 5 minutes (if using frozen, follow the packet cooking time) in a saucepan of boiling salted water or until tender, removing with a slotted spoon into iced water. The broad beans and asparagus can now be cooked together for just 2 to 3 minutes, also lifting from the water once tender and adding them to the iced peas. Once cold, drain off the water and skin the broad beans to reveal their rich green colour.

Heat a frying pan with the olive oil. Season the hake with salt and pepper and place, skin-side down, in the pan. Cook over a medium heat until the skin has become golden and crispy and the fish cooked half to two thirds of the way through. Add the knob of butter and turn the fish, removing the pan from the stove and basting the fillets with the butter.

While frying the fish, quickly microwave the ham, tear into thick strands and add to the white wine stock. Add the peas, beans and asparagus, stir in the butter and remove the bay leaf. Add the parsley, if using, and divide among four bowls, topping with the pan-fried hake.

more
- *This dish works just superbly with a poached egg, the yolk enriching the sauce (see page 24).*

serves four

2 large shallots, peeled and sliced into rings
1 glass of white wine
1 bay leaf
300ml (10fl oz) chicken stock (see note on page 8)
100g (4oz) peas, fresh and podded or frozen
100g (4oz) podded broad beans
8–12 asparagus spears, cut into 5–6cm (2–2½ inch) sticks
2 tablespoons olive oil
4 x 175g (6oz) hake fillets, skin on
salt and pepper
50g (2oz) butter, plus a knob of butter for the fish
100g (4oz) thick slice of ham
1 heaped tablespoon chopped flat-leaf parsley (optional)

a piece of salmon with roasted pine nut and lemon French beans

Heat a wok or frying pan, add the pine nuts and roast to a golden brown before tipping into a bowl. The nuts can be roughly chopped or left whole once cooked.

Season the salmon fillets with the sea salt and pepper. Heat a second frying pan over a medium heat with a splash of olive oil and a knob of the cold butter. Once sizzling, place the fillets in the pan skin-side down. Cook gently for 5 to 6 minutes to a light golden brown before turning them in the pan. Remove the pan from the heat and keep to one side.

Meanwhile, put another knob of the butter and splash of water in the first wok or frying pan. Over a fairly hot heat and when the butter and water are bubbling, add the beans, seasoning with a twist of pepper. Stir and cook for a few minutes until just tender. Add the pine nuts and a sprinkling of sea salt.

Arrange the salmon and roasted pine nut beans on four plates. Heat the lemon juice in the wok or frying pan and, once warm, whisk in the remaining butter. Sprinkle a pinch of sea salt over the salmon and beans, drizzling with the lemon-flavoured butter.

serves four

2 tablespoons pine nuts
4 x 175g (6oz) salmon fillets, skinned and pinboned
sea salt and pepper
olive oil, for cooking
75g (3oz) cold diced butter
225g (8oz) French beans, topped and tailed and thinly sliced at a slight angle
juice of 1 lemon

pan-fried sea bass with smoked bacon and caper cabbage

Dry the sea bass on kitchen paper, season with salt and pepper and lightly dust the skin with flour.

Heat the olive oil in a non-stick frying pan. Place the bass in the pan, skin-side down, lightly pressing with a fish slice to ensure all the skin is frying and colouring. The sea bass will take 5 to 7 minutes to crisp before you can turn it and remove from the heat. The residual warmth in the pan will continue the cooking process.

Meanwhile, plunge the shredded cabbage in boiling salted water and cook until just tender but leaving a slight bite, then drain.

While the cabbage is boiling, in a separate pan, fry the smoked bacon until golden brown. Add the cooked cabbage, capers and the knob of butter and season with a twist of pepper.

Arrange the cabbage on plates with the sea bass. Pour the lemon juice into the sea bass frying pan along with a tablespoon of water. Once simmering, stir in the butter until it has combined with the lemon juice and trickle it over the cabbage and bass.

more
• *Chopped chives can be added to the cabbage or lemon butter for a more oniony taste.*

serves four

4 x 175g (6oz) sea bass fillets, skin on
salt and pepper
flour, for dusting
olive oil, for cooking
½ savoy cabbage, finely shredded
4 rashers of smoked bacon, roughly chopped
2 tablespoons small capers
50g (2oz) cold chopped butter, plus a knob of butter for the cabbage
juice of ½ lemon

seared halibut with a blood orange and basil courgette salad

It's not essential to feature halibut in this recipe because so many other fish, such as turbot, tuna, brill, red mullet, scallops (or even chicken) will suit this salad perfectly.

To segment the blood oranges for the salad, top and tail the fruits using a serrated edged knife. The rind and pith can now be removed by cutting in a sawing motion down the sides. To release the segments, simply cut between each membrane, saving all of the juices.

Trim the ends of the courgettes and, with a Y-shaped potato peeler, slice lengthways into long, thin strips.

To make the dressing, boil the fresh orange juice along with any saved from the segments in a frying pan with the sugar until reduced in volume to 100ml (4fl oz). Once cool, whisk in the chosen oil and season with salt and pepper.

Pat dry the halibut on kitchen paper. Season with salt and pepper and lightly dust with flour.

Heat 2 to 3 tablespoons olive oil in a non-stick frying pan and fry the fillets over a medium heat for 5 to 8 minutes, depending on the thickness of the fish. Turn the fillets in the pan, adding the knob of butter. Once sizzling, add the lemon juice and begin to baste the fish for a minute before removing the pan from the heat.

Meanwhile, mix together in a bowl the orange segments, courgette strips, red onion and basil leaves, seasoning with sea salt and pepper. Add a few tablespoons of the dressing and gently stir it all together.

Divide the salad and halibut among the plates and drizzle with the remaining salad dressing to finish.

serves four

4 x 175g (6oz) halibut fillets, skinned
salt and pepper
flour, for dusting
olive oil, for cooking
a knob of butter
a squeeze of lemon juice

for the salad
3 blood oranges
4 small or 2 medium/large courgettes
1 red onion, thinly sliced
a handful of basil leaves, coarsely torn
coarse sea salt and pepper

for the dressing
200ml (7fl oz) fresh orange juice
½ teaspoon caster sugar
50ml (2fl oz) olive oil (or walnut oil for a nutty bite)
salt and pepper

stir-fried chicken with tomatoes, basil and crispy parmesan

Preheat the oven to 180°C/350°F/gas 4.

Mix together the cherry tomatoes, garlic and 4 tablespoons of the olive oil in a roasting tray and season with salt, pepper and a pinch of sugar.

Bake in the oven for 20 to 25 minutes until the tomatoes have softened and released their juices, creating a dressing with the olive oil.

While the 'cherries' are baking, divide the grated Parmesan into four circles on a non-stick baking tray and place in the oven for 10 to 12 minutes until the cheese has melted. Remove from the oven, and then leave to cool. The Parmesan will now have set into four crispy wafers.

Meanwhile, during the last 10 minutes of baking the tomatoes, season the chicken pieces with salt and pepper. Heat a wok or large frying pan with the remaining two tablespoons of olive oil. Once hot, fry the chicken, allowing the pieces to become a rich golden brown before adding the knob of butter and the sliced onion. The chicken and onion will take just 6 to 7 minutes to cook until tender. Finish with a squeeze of lemon juice, if using.

Divide the chicken among the plates or bowls, spooning over the soft cherry tomatoes. Sprinkle with the basil leaves and top with the crispy Parmesan wafers.

serves four

2 x 225g (8oz) punnets of cherry tomatoes, halved
2 cloves of garlic, chopped
6 tablespoons olive oil
sea salt and pepper
a pinch of sugar
100g (4oz) Parmesan cheese, grated
4 chicken breasts, skinned, each cut into 5 or 6 pieces
a knob of butter
1 onion, thinly sliced
a squeeze of lemon juice (optional)
a handful of small basil leaves

lemon and chilli sesame pork with mangetout

To precook the mangetout, snap away and discard the tops, plunging the vegetables into rapidly boiling salted water for 1 minute before draining and keeping to one side.

Heat a wok or frying pan, add the sesame seeds and 'toast' until golden brown. Spoon into a bowl and leave to one side.

Add a splash of olive oil to the pan and fry the shallots, chilli and lemon zest over a medium heat for a few minutes until the shallots are just beginning to soften.

Season the pork with salt and pepper. Increase the heat in the pan, add the pork and fry for just a few minutes until the pork is golden brown. Stir in the mangetout, sesame seeds, butter and lemon juice (using just half if it's a particularly juicy fruit). Finish with a trickle of sesame oil, if using.

more
• A dollop of natural yoghurt, crème fraîche or sour cream can be added or offered separately for a creamier dish.

serves two

100g (4oz) mangetout
2 teaspoons sesame seeds
olive oil, for cooking
2 shallots, peeled and sliced
2 medium red chillies, halved, deseeded and very thinly sliced
zest and juice of 1 lemon
350g (12oz) pork fillet or loin, sliced into thin strips
sea salt and pepper
a knob of butter
a trickle of sesame oil (optional)

roast chateaubriand with macaroni cheese

Chateaubriand is a cut taken from the top head end or centre of a beef fillet weighing 450g (1lb) or more. Once cut, it's usually batted until 4–5cm (1½–2 inches) thick to resemble a thick rib-eye steak and is cooked and carved for two. The sauce for the macaroni can be made with English Cheddar cheese or perhaps a Dutch Gouda.

Preheat the oven to 220°C/425°F/gas 7.

Heat the oil in an ovenproof frying pan. Once hot and smoking, season the chateaubriand with the sea salt and a twist of pepper and put in the pan. Fry until well coloured before turning and placing the pan in the oven. Roast for 4 to 5 minutes for rare and 8 to 10 minutes for medium, depending on thickness. Once cooked, remove the pan from the oven and allow the chateaubriand to rest for a few minutes.

While frying the steak, cook the macaroni in boiling salted water until tender but leaving a slight bite, then drain.

Warm together the single cream, crème fraîche and 100g (4oz) of the cheese over a gentle heat, not allowing the sauce to boil, until melted. Loosen with milk until a sauce consistency and season with salt and pepper. Mix the sauce with the macaroni. The extra cheese can be added for a stronger flavour or transfer the macaroni to an earthenware dish, sprinkle the remaining cheese over the top and colour under a preheated grill.

The chateaubriand can now be carved into even slices and served with a spoonful or two of the macaroni.

more
- *A teaspoon of English or Dijon mustard can be added to the cheese sauce.*

serves two

2 tablespoons vegetable oil
1 beef chateaubriand (see left)
sea salt and pepper
200g (7oz) macaroni

for the cheese sauce
150ml (5fl oz) single cream
100g (4oz) crème fraîche
100–150g (4–5oz) cheese, grated (see left)
a splash of milk
salt and pepper

spiced lamb escalopes with mango, apple and cucumber salad

The mango, apple and cucumber can be chopped or sliced. If chopped, the salad is best bound with the mint yoghurt. If sliced, drizzle the yoghurt over the fruit and salad leaves.

Cut away the bone from each lamb steak and, using a meat tenderizer, bat the steaks into large escalopes between 5 to 10mm (¼–½ inch) thick. Season with salt and pepper.

Whisk together in a bowl 2 tablespoons of the yoghurt, the juice of ½ lime, the curry powder and garlic. Dip and coat the escalopes in the mix, leaving to infuse while the salad is prepared.

Cut away the mango flesh from the stone, dividing each half into quarters before removing the skin. The mango, along with the apple and cucumber, can now be sliced or chopped.

Whisk the remaining yoghurt, lime juice and mint together, seasoning with salt and pepper.

Heat the cooking oil in a large frying pan. Once hot, fry the yoghurt-covered lamb escalopes for 3 to 5 minutes on each side, depending on their thickness, maintaining a pink centre. Remove from the heat and allow to rest.

Meanwhile, arrange the fruit, cucumber and salad leaves on the plates and drizzle over with the yoghurt and mint dressing. Arrange the escalopes next to the salads and serve.

serves two

2 x 175–200g (6–7oz) leg of lamb steaks
salt and pepper
150ml (5fl oz) natural yoghurt
juice 1 lime
1 teaspoon medium curry powder
1 small clove of garlic, peeled and finely chopped
1 mango
1 apple, cored
¼ cucumber, peeled
1 heaped tablespoon chopped mint
2 tablespoons vegetable oil
1–2 handfuls of salad leaves

risotto milanese

This risotto is an Italian classic, flavoured with saffron and usually served with osso buco (see page 200), but it works equally well on its own as a supper dish. For this recipe I've chosen carnaroli, the premier risotto rice, but arborio or vialone nano can also be used. Not all of the stock may be needed. However, I feel that a little too much is better than not enough.

serves four

1.5 litres (2½ pints) chicken or vegetable stock (see note on page 8)
100g (4oz) butter
1 onion, very finely chopped
350g (12oz) carnaroli rice
a generous pinch of saffron strands
150ml (5fl oz) white wine
salt and pepper
50g (2oz) Parmesan cheese, grated

Bring your chosen stock to the boil and turn down the heat to a gentle simmer.

Melt half the butter in a heavy-based pan. Add the chopped onion and cook gently, without colouring, for 6 to 7 minutes until softened.

Sprinkle in the rice and stir to make sure the grains are coated in the butter. Stir the saffron strands into the wine, pour in and continue to cook until the wine has been totally absorbed.

Stir in one or two ladlefuls of hot stock and cook over a medium heat, stirring continuously. Once almost completely evaporated, add another couple of ladlefuls and continue this process for 17 to 20 minutes. The risotto is ready when the rice grains are tender, but are left with the slightest of bites.

Stir in the remaining butter so that the risotto texture and consistency is reasonably loose and creamy, but not too wet. Season with salt and pepper and finish with a good sprinkling of the Parmesan, offering any remaining on the side.

more
- *Veal or beef marrow can be added, melting it with the butter before cooking the onion. The marrow adds extra richness to the overall flavour.*

ready in 30 to 60 minutes

ready in 30 to 60 minutes

The recipes in this chapter are something a bit special. Gone are the short cuts and concise ingredients lists of earlier chapters because, with a little forethought, I think something truly wonderful can be cooked and on the table in under an hour.

With a little extra time, 60 minutes gives you the chance to bring two fully developed ideas to the plate. Seared black bream with ginger, tomato and chilli pak choy or cumberland sausages and onions with three-cheese glazed spinach match two elements together to produce a symphony of flavour. Of course, the 'ready in 30 minutes' cook could borrow just the potatoes from the sharp lime skate with crème fraîche jersey royals and put them with perhaps some butcher's sausages, but the 'ready in 60 minutes' cook has time to create that extra layer of flavour that can make a dish even more memorable.

With a whole hour to savour, I've introduced some new ingredients here: duck, crab, mussels, calves' liver and even guinea fowl. Some of these can, of course, be cooked in no time at all, but less familiar to most cooks, their preparation, garnishes and accompaniments do perhaps require a bit more time and consideration.

Cooking a dish in under 60 minutes doesn't mean an hour of furious chopping and stirring. Making food has a rhythm to it and that means pauses as well as bursts of activity. My honey, lemon and thyme roast chicken barely fits into this chapter with exactly an hour of roasting, but once the chicken is in the oven, your job is simply to occasionally baste with butter.

The food in this chapter is not rustic, peasant food, you need a lot more time to cook the rich stews and braises we associate with that style of cooking, but it is food that looks and tastes outstanding. These recipes are particularly attractive and would, I think, shine as part of any special dinner for family or friends.

beef tomato and aubergine cottage pie

There are two stages to this recipe, making reference to others within the book. The mashed potato quantity is more than generous to top the tomatoes, but an extra dollop is rarely refused. The cheese sauce from page 114 acts as the moistener between the aubergine layers and leaves enough for a spoonful or two to be drizzled over once cooked.

Preheat the oven to 190°C/375°F/gas 5.

Remove the eye from the tomatoes before slicing off the round top of each. Cut around the centre seeds with a small knife to loosen before scooping all of the seeds clear. Season the tomatoes with salt and pepper and place on a baking tray.

Slice each of the aubergines into six. Heat the olive oil in a frying pan or two and pan-fry the aubergine slices over a medium heat for 3 to 4 minutes on each side until golden brown. Remove the slices from the pan and keep to one side. Season with salt and pepper.

Warm the butter in the pan. Once bubbling, add the sliced spring onion, stirring once or twice before removing from the pan.

Spoon two teaspoons of the cheese sauce into the base of each tomato and top with an aubergine slice and a sprinkling of spring onion. Repeat with more sauce and onions, finishing with a last slice of aubergine. As the layers are built, gently press to create a smooth finish along the top of the tomatoes. Top each with mashed potatoes, either piping or spreading before sprinkling with Parmesan, if using.

Bake for 20 to 25 minutes until heated through and the potato has slightly coloured. The tomatoes are now ready to serve, offering any extra warm cheese sauce separately.

serves four

4 beef tomatoes
salt and pepper
2 small aubergines
3 tablespoons olive oil
a small knob of butter
6 spring onions, finely sliced
1 x cheese sauce
  (see page 114)
1 x mashed potatoes
  (see page 142)
2 tablespoons finely grated
  Parmesan (optional)

tuna carpaccio with mustard split beans and red onions

It's important that the tuna is very fresh and purchased as one whole piece of fillet. For thin, even slices, the fillet is best placed in the freezer for 30 to 60 minutes to firm up and make it easier to slice.

Blanch the French beans in boiling salted water for a few minutes until tender, but still maintaining a bite. Refresh in iced water and drain. The beans can now be split lengthways in half.

In a bowl, mix together the Dijon mustard and red wine vinegar with a generous squeeze of lemon. Slowly whisk in the olive oil until the dressing has combined. Season with salt and pepper

Mix together the split beans, red onion and parsley and stir in the mustard dressing to coat. Any extra can be drizzled over the carpaccio on the plates. Season with sea salt and a generous twist of pepper.

Using a shape knife or mandolin, cut the par-frozen tuna into very thin slices. Four plates or a platter can now be covered with the sliced fish and scattered with the mustard split beans and red onion, or the slices can be laid on top of the beans and red onion mixture.

more
- *A dollop of natural yoghurt added to the mustard before making the dressing will give a creamy and slightly milder flavour.*
- *If you're left with half a lemon, divide into quarters and serve with the tuna.*

serves four

350g (12oz) French beans, topped
2 teaspoons Dijon mustard
1 tablespoon red wine vinegar
a squeeze of lemon juice
50ml (2fl oz) olive oil
sea salt and pepper
1 red onion, thinly sliced
a handful of torn flat-leaf parsley leaves
225g (8oz) chilled tuna (see left)

goujons of smoked eel with horseradish cream

This dish could probably be made within 20 to 30 minutes, but finds its way into this chapter to help the flavours in the horseradish sauce blend and develop to their full strength. I've kept this recipe simply as goujons with a sauce dip, however golden crispy eel fingers scattered over a salad of mixed leaves and beetroot is equally good.

To make the horseradish cream, add the vinegar, mustard and sugar to the double cream and whisk until soft peaks form. Stir in the horseradish and season with salt and pepper.

Cut the smoked eel into approximately 7cm x 1cm (2¾ inch x ½ inch) sticks. Season the flour with salt and pepper. Lightly dust a handful of eel sticks at a time in the flour, then coat in the egg and breadcrumbs. Continue with the remainder, keeping the goujons separate to prevent them from becoming soggy.

Heat the oil in a large pan or deep-fat fryer to 180°–190°C (350–375°F) and fry a handful of eel sticks for 1 to 2 minutes until a light golden brown. Using a slotted spoon, lift the goujons from the oil on to a kitchen-paper-lined plate. Once the oil has returned to the correct temperature, fry the remainder.

Stack a plate or bowl with the eel goujons and serve with the horseradish cream and lemon wedges.

more
- *The fresh horseradish can be replaced by horseradish from a jar, adding a tablespoon at a time to your taste. The vinegar can also be swapped with lemon juice and the double cream with crème fraîche.*

serves four–six

450g (1lb) smoked eel fillet
flour, for dusting
salt and pepper
2 eggs, beaten
100g (4oz) fresh or dried
  white breadcrumbs
vegetable oil, for deep-frying
4 wedges of lemon

for the horseradish cream
1 tablespoon white wine
  vinegar
1 teaspoon English mustard
a pinch of caster sugar
150ml (5fl oz) double cream
50g (2oz) fresh horseradish,
  peeled and finely grated
salt and pepper

spiced crème fraîche mussels with a nutty mango and cos heart salad

The spicy edge to the crème fraîche is curry paste, the paste and cream simmered together in this recipe with the mussel juices. The nuts are cashews, although almonds or hazelnuts also work well, and I've selected small cos for the salad, using mostly the heart leaves.

To clean the mussels, scrub the shells in cold water, scraping off any barnacles and pulling away the beards. If any mussels are slightly open, a short, sharp tap should make them close, letting you know they are still alive. Any that don't close should be discarded.

Heat a large saucepan on top of the stove. Add the mussels with a few tablespoons of water. Cover with a lid and cook over a high heat for 3 to 5 minutes, shaking the pan and stirring the mussels from time to time until the shells have opened.

Strain in a colander, saving all of the juices except the last couple of tablespoons, which tend to be gritty. Once slightly cooled, remove the mussels from their shells, discarding any that have not opened.

Warm 100ml (3½fl oz) of the saved mussel juices and whisk in the curry paste. Simmer for a few minutes before whisking in the crème fraîche. Season with salt and pepper, if needed.

Scatter the cos leaves, chopped cashew nuts and chopped mango in the centre of the serving plates. Quickly warm the mussels in the spicy crème fraîche sauce, stir in the chopped chives and spoon over the leaves, nuts and mango. Drizzle with a drop or two of olive oil and a squeeze of lime.

serves four

1kg (2¼lb) mussels
1 teaspoon medium curry paste
100g (4oz) crème fraîche
salt and pepper
2 small cos lettuces, leaves separated
75g (3oz) unsalted roasted cashew nuts, roughly chopped
2 small mangoes or 1 large, peeled and chopped
1 tablespoon finely chopped chives
olive oil, for drizzling
1 lime, quartered

seared black bream with ginger, tomato and chilli pak choy

Sesame oil can be used in place of the olive, perhaps half and half with groundnut oil to prevent the dressing from becoming too strong.

Shred the pak choy into 5–10mm (¼–½ inch) slices or simply cut into halves or thin wedges. Boil a saucepan of salted water and quickly plunge in the pak choy. Stir once or twice and then drain in a colander, reserving the water.

The boiling water can now be used to blanch the tomatoes. With the point of a knife, remove the eye from the tomatoes. Cut a cross in the skin on each base and plunge into the water for 10 to 15 seconds before placing under cold running water. Once cold, the skin peels away easily. Peel, quarter and deseed before cutting into 5–10mm (¼–½ inch) cubes.

Peel the ginger, slice thinly and cut into very thin strips. Whisk together 2 tablespoons of the olive oil with the lime juice and honey, stirring in the red chilli, ginger, spring onion and tomato. Season with salt and pepper.

Meanwhile, heat a frying pan with the remaining olive oil. Season the black bream with salt and pepper and place skin-side down in the pan. Fry over a medium-high heat for 4 to 5 minutes, adding a knob of butter. Once sizzling, turn the fish and remove the pan from the stove, basting the bream with the butter.

While frying the fish, heat a wok or frying pan. Sprinkle in the sesame seeds and once they reach a golden brown, add the remaining knob of butter and the pak choy. Season with salt and pepper and fry for a few minutes to heat through.

Arrange the pak choy on a plate, spooning the dressing over and around. Top with the black beam and serve.

serves four

450g (1lb) pak choy
3 plum tomatoes
3–4cm (1¼–1½ inch) piece of
fresh ginger
3 tablespoons olive oil
juice of 1 lime
1 teaspoon honey
1 mild fresh red chilli, sliced
into rings (discard the
seeds for a milder taste)
2 spring onions, thinly sliced
salt and pepper
4 x 175g (6oz) black bream
fillets
2 knobs of butter
1 tablespoon sesame seeds

sharp lime skate with crème fraîche jersey royals

It's not essential to use Jersey Royals in this recipe, but they do offer the richest of buttery and creamy flavours.

Cook the Jersey Royals in boiling salted water until slightly overcooked (15 to 20 minutes if small and 20 to 25 minutes if large).

Once cooked, drain and cut each potato in half. Season with salt and pepper, adding a squeeze of lemon juice and a sprinkling of olive oil. Keep the potatoes warm and to one side.

Peel two of the limes, removing all the zest and pith before cutting between each membrane into segments. Halve the segments.

Heat the remaining olive oil in a large non-stick frying pan. Season the skate wings and place in the pan. Fry for 4 to 5 minutes until golden brown before turning and removing the pan from the heat. The fish will continue cooking in the pan.

Spoon the baby spinach leaves, if using, into the warm potatoes. Once the leaves begin to wilt, stir in the crème fraîche, using all of it for a soft, creamy dressing. Season with salt and pepper.

Divide the potatoes among the plates along with the skate fillets.

Reheat the frying pan and add the juice of the remaining lime along with 1 tablespoon water. Once simmering, whisk in the butter, adding the final 25g (1oz) for a smooth, silky finish.

Add the halved lime segments and chopped chives to the butter sauce and spoon over the skate.

serves four

- 450g (1lb) Jersey Royal potatoes
- sea salt and pepper
- a squeeze of lemon juice
- a sprinkling of olive oil, plus 2 tablespoons extra for cooking
- 3 limes
- 4 x 175g (6oz) skate wings, filleted and skinned and cut into 3 strips
- a handful or two (approximately 100–150g/4–5oz) of washed baby spinach leaves (optional)
- 3–4 generous tablespoons crème fraîche
- 50–75g (2–3oz) butter
- 1 tablespoon chopped chives

red mullet with avocado niçoise salad

Niçoise has become a common title found in many cookery books. It seems that it's a classic that will never die. Here's another adaptation that is very simple to create with lots of flavour and colour.

Cook the new potatoes in boiling salted water for 15 to 20 minutes until tender. Drain and keep warm to one side. While cooking the potatoes, the eggs can be boiled for 7 to 8 minutes (or just 3 minutes if you're using quail's eggs), before plunging into cold water for a minute or two and then shelling.

Cook the French beans for 2 to 3 minutes in rapidly boiling water, then put into iced water to refresh and drain once chilled.

Peel the avocados before halving, removing the stone and cutting each half into four. Drizzle with the juice of half the lime.

For the vinaigrette, mix together the mustard, vinegar and sugar, then whisk in the olive oil and remaining half of the lime juice. Season with salt and pepper.

Heat a non-stick frying pan with a splash or two of olive oil. Season the mullet fillets with salt and pepper and place them in the pan skin-side down. Fry over a medium heat for 5 to 6 minutes (7 to 8 minutes if using large fillets), adding the knob of butter. Once bubbling, turn the fillets and remove the pan from the heat. The residual heat in the pan continues the cooking process, leaving a moist, almost pink centre in the fish.

Meanwhile, in a large bowl, mix together all of the salad ingredients, halving the new potatoes as you add them and including the capers and anchovy fillets, if using. Drizzle over the vinaigrette and divide the salad on to four plates along with the mullet fillets.

serves four

8 new potatoes
4 eggs or 12 quail's eggs
100g (4oz) French beans, topped
2 avocados
1 lime
olive oil, for cooking
2 x red mullet, scaled, filleted and pinboned (450g each)
salt and pepper
a knob of butter
2 little gems, leaves separated
175g (6oz) cherry tomatoes, halved
16–20 stoned black olives
1 tablespoon capers (optional)
12 marinated anchovy fillets (optional)

for the vinaigrette
1 teaspoon Dijon mustard
2 tablespoons white wine vinegar
pinch of sugar
6 tablespoons olive oil
salt and pepper

sea bass with tomatoes, crab and fresh herbs

To make the creamy mayonnaise, mix together the mayonnaise, garlic and lemon juice. Lightly whip the cream to a soft peak and fold into the mayonnaise. Season with salt and pepper. The sauce can now be refrigerated, removing it 5 to 10 minutes before serving.

Pick through the crabmeat, discarding any shell splinters. Using a sharp knife, score four to five lines in the skin of each sea bass fillet to help prevent the fillets from curling in the pan.

Warm a frying pan with 2 tablespoons of the olive oil over a medium heat. Season the fish with sea salt and pepper and put the fillets in the pan, skin-side down. Fry for 6 to 7 minutes until crispy, add the butter and, once sizzling, turn the fish in the pan and remove from the heat. The residual heat in the pan will continue the cooking process.

Heat 3 tablespoons of the olive oil in another frying pan. Once warmed, add the shallot rings and sugar, frying for a few minutes until just beginning to soften. Increase the heat and add the cherry tomatoes. Once softening, stir in the crabmeat and fresh herbs, seasoning with salt and pepper.

Spoon the tomatoes, crab and herbs onto plates, topping with the sea bass and serving the creamy mayonnaise separately.

more
- *A squeeze of the remaining lemon half can be added to the tomatoes.*

serves six

100g (4oz) fresh white crabmeat
6 x 175g (6oz) sea bass fillets, skin on
5 tablespoons olive oil
sea salt and pepper
a knob of butter
4 shallots, peeled and sliced into rings
a pinch of sugar
500g (18oz) cherry tomatoes, halved
a generous handful of mixed chervil, flat-leaf parsley, tarragon and basil, roughly chopped
1 tablespoon chopped chives

for the creamy mayonnaise
150g (5oz) mayonnaise
2 cloves of garlic, puréed
juice of ½ lemon
100ml (3½fl oz) double cream
salt and pepper

roast sea trout with spinach, orange and crushed new potatoes

Cook the new potatoes in boiling salted water for 30 minutes until overcooked. Drain the potatoes and keep warm in the saucepan, topped with a lid to one side.

Meanwhile, to make the sauce, top and tail the orange. The rind and pith can now be removed by cutting in a sawing motion down the sides. To release the segments, cut between each membrane, saving all the juice.

Place the chopped shallot and white wine in a saucepan and boil until just one quarter of the liquid is left. Add the saved orange juice and continue to boil until one third of the liquid is left before stirring in the cream. Remove from the heat and keep to one side.

Heat a frying pan with a drop of olive oil. Season the sea trout with salt and pepper and put in the pan, skin-side down. Fry over a medium-hot heat for 6 to 7 minutes, allowing the skin to crisp and roast. Turn the fish in the pan and remove from the heat. The residual heat in the pan will continue the cooking process.

While frying the sea trout, heat a saucepan with a knob of butter, drop in the spinach leaves and stir around the pan for a few minutes until wilted and tender. Season.

When ready to serve, use a fork to gently crush the warm new potatoes with the 50g (2oz) butter and some sea salt and pepper, leaving a coarse texture.

Warm the sauce, whisking in the last knob of butter and half the orange segments, allowing them to break into strands as you whisk. The remaining segments can be used to garnish the fish. Divide the spinach, crushed potatoes and trout among four plates and pour the orange sauce over the top.

serves four

1kg (2¼lb) new potatoes
olive oil, for cooking
4 x 175g (6oz) sea trout fillets, skin on
sea salt and pepper
50g (2oz) butter, plus 1 extra knob
900g (2lb) spinach, stalks removed and washed

for the orange sauce
1 orange
1 shallot or small onion, finely chopped
1 glass of white wine
2 tablespoons double or whipping cream
a knob of butter

pan-fried brill with white wine, capers, lemon and mashed potatoes

For me, this is a complete meal, but if you want veg to go with it, steamed spinach is probably your best bet.

Cook the potatoes in boiling salted water for 20 to 25 minutes until tender. Drain well, replace the lid and shake vigorously to break up the potatoes. Mash by hand or using a potato ricer. Mix really well for a smooth finish, adding the butter and cream until the potatoes are soft, light and creamy. Season with salt and ground white pepper. Keep warm to one side.

Heat a frying pan with the olive oil and season the fish with salt and pepper. When hot, place the brill fillets, skinned-side down, in the pan. Fry for 1 to 2 minutes until golden brown. Transfer the fillets onto a plate and keep to one side, ready to be finished in the sauce.

Pour away any remaining oil in the pan and return it to the stove. Increase the heat, pour in the white wine and boil until there are just a few tablespoons left. Add the stock and return to the boil, evaporating until just half the liquid is left.

Squeeze in the juice of ½ lemon, adding extra for a sharper taste. Add the capers and stir in the butter for a silky consistency. Season with salt and pepper and return the brill to the pan, fried-side up. Simmer gently for 1 minute and sprinkle with the chopped parsley.

The brill is now ready to serve with the creamy mashed potatoes.

serves four

for the mash
900g (2lb) floury potatoes, such as Maris Piper or King Edwards, peeled and quartered
75g (3oz) butter
100–150ml (3½–5fl oz) single cream or milk
salt and ground white pepper

for the brill
2 tablespoons olive oil
4 x 150–175g (5–6oz) brill fillets, skinned
salt and pepper
100ml (3½fl oz) white wine
200ml (7fl oz) chicken stock (see note on page 8)
1 lemon, halved
2 tablespoons small capers, rinsed
50g (2oz) butter
1 heaped tablespoon chopped flat-leaf parsley

half chestnut guinea fowl

A simple recipe with half a roast guinea fowl each, a spoonful of spring greens and lots of chestnut mushrooms strewn across the top.

Preheat the oven to 200°C/400°F/gas 6.

Place the guinea fowl in a roasting tin, seasoning with salt and pepper. Trickle with a little oil and roast in the oven for 50 minutes, basting from time to time. Once cooked, remove the bird from the oven and leave to rest for 5 to 10 minutes.

Meanwhile, tear the spring green leaves into bite-sized pieces and blanch in boiling salted water for 2 to 3 minutes until tender. Refresh quickly in a bowl of iced water before draining and gently squeezing to release excess water. Season with salt, pepper and freshly grated nutmeg, if using. When you're ready to eat, the greens can be quickly reheated with a knob of butter in a microwave or warmed in a saucepan.

While the bird is resting, heat a large frying pan or wok with just a dot of olive oil. When very hot, add the chestnut mushrooms, allowing them to almost dry-fry over a high heat. Season with salt and pepper, stirring from time to time until well coloured. Stir in the butter, mixing it with any mushroom juices collected in the pan.

Cut the legs and breast from the bird and reheat the spring greens. Spoon the greens onto two plates along with a half guinea fowl and the chestnut mushrooms. Any saved roasting juices can be drizzled over the top.

serves two

1 guinea fowl (approximately 1.25kg/2½lb)
salt and pepper
olive oil, for cooking
350g (12oz) spring greens, stalks removed and washed
freshly grated nutmeg (optional)
25g (1oz) butter, plus an extra knob
400g (14oz) chestnut mushrooms, thickly sliced
a squeeze of lemon (optional)

honey, lemon and thyme roast chicken

This recipe only just fits into this chapter with the roasting time at exactly 1 hour. Once cooked, the bird needs to rest to allow the meat to relax. Here, the chicken relaxes while still in the oven after simply switching the oven off.

Preheat the oven to 200°C/400°F/gas 6.

Rub the chicken all over with the butter and season liberally with the salt and pepper.

Place the chicken in a roasting tray and pop into the oven, leaving to roast for 40 minutes. At this point, remove the bird from the oven, pour away any juices into a bowl and return the bird to the tray.

Mix together the lemon zest, thyme leaves and honey and pour it over the chicken before returning it to the oven. Every 5 minutes or so, baste the chicken with the honey mixture. After 20 minutes, baste once more and turn off the oven, leaving the chicken to rest in the oven for 15 minutes.

Remove the sticky honey chicken from the roasting tray. Heat all of the honey and saved juices together in the tray with a little water to loosen, if needed.

Meanwhile, remove the legs from the chicken, separating the thigh and drumstick, and carve the breast into thick slices. Divide the chicken on to four plates, spooning over the simmering honey, lemon and thyme juices.

serves four

1.6–1.8kg (3½–4lb) chicken
butter, for roasting
sea salt and pepper
finely grated zest of 1 lemon
1 level tablespoon picked
    thyme leaves
4 tablespoons clear honey

roast chicken breasts with almond cream noodles

Preheat the oven to 180°C/350°F/gas 4.

To make the sauce, scatter the almonds on to a baking tray and toast in the oven until golden brown.

Boil together the chopped shallots and white wine, reducing in volume until just three quarters of the liquid is left. Add in the chicken stock, stir in the double cream and toasted flaked almonds (a few can be kept to sprinkle on top), then simmer the sauce for 5 to 10 minutes until the sauce has slightly thickened. Remove from the heat and leave to cool for 10 minutes before liquidizing in a blender until smooth. To remove any slight grain caused by the almonds, strain through a fine sieve.

Meanwhile, season the chicken with sea salt and pepper. Heat a roasting tray with a splash or two of olive oil. Put the breasts, skin-side down, in the tray and fry on the stove top for 5 to 7 minutes until a rich golden brown. Turn the breasts in the tray, adding the knob of butter. Once melted, baste the chicken with the butter and roast in the oven for a further 8 to 10 minutes until firm to the touch. Once cooked, baste the chicken over and over with the butter and any juices to enrich its flavour.

While roasting the chicken, the pasta can be cooked in boiling salted water until tender but leaving a slight bite, then drain well in a colander and return the pasta to the pan.

Stir the almond cream sauce into the noodles and they are now ready to serve with the chicken, sprinkling any saved toasted almond flakes over the pasta.

serves four

4 chicken breasts, skin on
sea salt and pepper
olive oil, for cooking
a knob of butter
400g (14oz) tagliatelle

for the sauce
50g (2oz) flaked almonds
2 shallots, finely chopped
1 glass of white wine
300ml (10fl oz) chicken stock
  (see note on page 8)
200ml (7fl oz) double cream

salt and pepper baby chickens with a red wine vinaigrette and lemon butter

Classically, this dish is cooked on an open wood fire grill. The alternative I'm using here is a grill pan, which does help create those burnt bitter edges. If you don't have one, try using a heavy-based frying pan or roast in a very hot oven. The backbone of the chickens needs to be removed and this can be done by simply cutting either side of it with a sharp pair of scissors. The birds can now be flattened, breast-side up, using the palm of your hand. To help maintain this shape, a wooden skewer can be pierced through the thigh and point of the breast. To accompany, you simply need a bowl of tossed green leaves.

serves two

2 shallots, finely chopped
finely grated zest and juice of 1 lemon
50g (2oz) butter, softened
sea salt and pepper
2 baby chickens (poussins), backbones removed and flattened (see left)
4 tablespoons olive oil
2 teaspoons red wine vinegar

Put the shallots, lemon zest and juice in a saucepan. Bring to the boil and allow the juice to evaporate until almost dry. Leave to cool. Once cool, mix in the butter and season with salt and pepper.

Preheat a grill pan or frying pan. Season the flattened baby chickens generously on both sides with salt and pepper. Drizzle a tablespoon of olive oil over each and press down, breast-side down, on the grill pan. Cook over a medium heat for 15 minutes before turning, reducing the heat slightly and continuing to grill for a further 15 to 20 minutes until cooked through. To test, pierce the thigh with the point of a sharp knife. Once the juices run clear, the chickens are cooked. If still slightly pink, continue to grill the birds for a further 5 to 10 minutes before presenting on plates.

Whisk together the remaining olive oil with the red wine vinegar and season with salt and pepper. Drizzle the dressing liberally over the birds and spoon a dollop of the lemon butter on top of each one.

roast duck breasts with spinach, wild mushrooms and maple syrup vinaigrette

Although the duck breasts are not actually roasted, simply pan-fried, the secret is to allow some of the duck fat to melt away, leaving a golden brown roasted colour and flavour.

Score the duck breast skin with a sharp knife. Season the breasts with salt and pepper and place, fat-side down, in a frying pan over a medium heat. As the fat begins to heat it will melt and crisp up. Continue to colour the skin for 10 to 12 minutes before turning the duck over and frying for a further 4 to 5 minutes to a pink stage. Remove the duck breasts and keep warm to one side.

Meanwhile, boil the maple syrup and simmer until just 2 tablespoons are left before removing from the heat and whisking in the sherry vinegar, groundnut and hazelnut oil. Season with salt and pepper.

While frying the duck breasts, trim and lightly rinse the wild mushrooms. When the duck is resting, fry the mushrooms in half the butter in a hot pan, seasoning with salt and pepper, until just tender.

Heat a separate pan with the remaining butter and add the washed spinach. Season with salt and pepper, allowing the leaves to wilt and soften before draining.

To serve, divide the spinach among four plates. Cut each breast into five to six slices and place on top of the spinach. Top with the pan-fried wild mushrooms, drizzling each with the maple syrup vinaigrette.

more
- *Once the fat side is coloured, the duck breasts can be finished off in a preheated 200°C/400°F/gas 6 oven for 4 to 5 minutes, creating extra cooking space on the stove.*

serves four

4 duck breasts, skin on
sea salt and pepper
4 tablespoons maple syrup
1½ tablespoons sherry
   vinegar
1½ tablespoons groundnut oil
1 tablespoon hazelnut oil
225g (8oz) wild mushrooms
   (girolles, trompettes, ceps,
   oyster mushrooms)
25g (1oz) butter
900g (2lb) spinach, stalks
   removed

warm gammon and pineapple with sour cream english leaves

I've chosen simple English salad leaves and featured cos, a round lettuce, little gem and watercress. The flavours and texture remain refreshing and crisp next to the rich gammon and pineapple.

Tear the salad leaves into a salad spinner or colander, rinsing lightly and leaving to drain.

To prepare the pineapple, cut off the top and bottom and trim away the coarse skin. Chop the fruit into roughly 1cm (½ inch) cubes, discarding the central core.

Heat a large non-stick frying pan. Once hot, add the pineapple, sprinkling with the sugar. Fry quickly over a high heat, allowing the sugar to lightly caramelize before seasoning with the sea salt and a generous twist of black pepper.

Pour the pineapple juice over the pineapple and bring to a simmer. As the fruit cooks, the syrup will begin to thicken. After a few minutes, drain the pineapple in a sieve over a bowl and keep the fruit to one side. The sour cream can now be whisked into the syrup in the bowl, seasoning if needed. For a slightly sharper taste, add a squeeze of lime or splash of balsamic vinegar.

Reheat the frying pan and add the oil. Once hot, the gammon can be quickly pan-fried for a few minutes until tender and golden brown. Season with salt and pepper and finish with a knob of butter.

Add the pineapple chunks to the gammon and place on a large plate. Sprinkle over the salad leaves, drizzling liberally with the pineapple-flavoured sour cream.

serves four

for the salad
1 small cos
1 small round lettuce
1 little gem
1 small bunch of watercress

1 small ripe pineapple
2 tablespoons light soft brown sugar
sea salt and pepper
100ml (3½fl oz) pineapple juice
150ml (5fl oz) sour cream
a squeeze of lime or splash of balsamic vinegar (optional)
1 tablespoon sunflower or groundnut oil
2 x 175–225g (6–8oz) gammon steaks (smoked or unsmoked), cut into 1cm (½ inch) thick strips or cubes
a knob of butter

burnt lamb chops with sweet peppers and onions

Preheat the grill. Put the whole red peppers under the hot grill and allow them to reach a deep, almost burnt, colour before turning and repeating until completely coloured. The peppers can now be peeled while still warm or placed in a plastic bag and left to cool before peeling. Once peeled, halve the peppers, cutting away the stalk and removing the seeds, and cut into thick strips.

Meanwhile, heat a large frying pan with 2 tablespoons of olive oil. Add the onion and fry over a medium heat until beginning to soften and colour. Season with salt and pepper and sprinkle over the caster sugar. Increase the heat and continue frying until the sugar begins to caramelize and the onion is a rich golden brown. Stir in the sweet peppers and the mix is now ready to use or to warm up when needed.

Quickly whisk the mint jelly into the crème fraîche with the chopped mint. Season with salt and pepper.

To cook the chops, heat a grill pan or frying pan. Once very hot, brush each chop lightly with olive oil and season with salt and pepper. Put the cutlets on the grill pan or in the frying pan, fat-side down. This will allow some of the fat to melt as it cooks, leaving a burnt and bitter edge to the lamb. Once well coloured, turn the chops on their sides and continue to cook over a high heat for a few minutes on each side, again to create a burnt edge.

Arrange the chops with the warm sweet peppers and onion, offering the mint crème fraîche separately.

more
* A simple green salad is all this dish needs to accompany it.

serves four

2 large red peppers
olive oil, for cooking
2 large onions, sliced
salt and pepper
2 teaspoons caster sugar
2 heaped teaspoons
  mint jelly
150g (5 oz) crème fraîche
1 tablespoon chopped mint
  leaves
8 lamb chops

fillet of beef with red wine tomatoes and bacon sauté potatoes

Cook the new potatoes in boiling salted water for 20 minutes until tender. Once cooked and drained, leave to cool before slicing in half lengthways ready to be sautéed.

Meanwhile, to make the tomato sauce, heat the olive oil in a wok or large frying pan. Add the onion and fry over a medium heat until golden brown. Once softened, add the sugar and continue to fry for a further few minutes before pouring in half of the red wine. Increase the heat and simmer until just a third of the liquid is left before adding half the chopped tomatoes, including the tomato juices. Continue to boil and repeat this process once more with the remaining wine, simmering again until just a third of the liquid is left. Pour in the last of the tomatoes, simmer rapidly until the sauce is thick and syrupy. Season with salt and pepper. Transfer the sauce to a saucepan and wipe the frying pan clean.

Preheat the oven to 220°C/425°F/gas 7.

Return the pan to the heat. Once hot, add the strips of streaky bacon, frying over a high heat until golden brown. Pan-fry the new potatoes until golden, adding the butter to help colour and enrich their flavour. Season with salt and pepper and sprinkle with chopped parsley, if using.

Meanwhile, heat an ovenproof frying pan with the remaining olive oil. Season the steaks with salt and pepper and fry until they are seared and well coloured all over. Add the butter and, once sizzling, turn the steaks before placing in the oven for 4 to 5 minutes for rare or 7 to 8 minutes for medium. Once cooked, remove from the oven and leave to rest in a warm place for 5 minutes. To serve, top each of the steaks with the red wine tomatoes and add a spoonful or two of the potatoes.

serves four

1–2 tablespoons olive oil
4 x 175g (6oz) fillet steaks, taken from the centre of the fillet
salt and pepper
a knob of butter

for the sauté potatoes
600g (1lb 5oz) new potatoes
8 rashers of streaky bacon, cut into 1cm (½ inch) strips
25g (1oz) butter
sea salt and pepper
1 heaped tablespoon chopped flat-leaf parsley (optional)

for the red wine tomato sauce
2 tablespoons olive oil
2 onions, thinly sliced
a pinch of sugar
300ml (10fl oz) red wine
400g (14oz) tin of chopped tomatoes
salt and pepper

cumberland sausages and onions with three-cheese glazed spinach

Two of the cheeses, the mozzarella and Cheddar, become a rich creamy sauce, while the third, the slices of Gruyère, are glazed on the top.

Heat a large frying pan with the olive oil. Once warm, add the sausages and fry gently over a medium heat for 20 to 25 minutes, turning for an even all-round colour. Remove the sausages from the pan and keep warm to one side.

Add the onion to the pan, increase the heat and fry for 5 to 7 minutes until a light golden brown and softening.

Warm the single cream and crème fraîche together in a saucepan. Once at a soft simmer, stir in the Cheddar cheese and mozzarella, warming over a low heat, but not allowing the sauce to boil. If too thick, loosen with a drop or two of milk. Season with salt and pepper.

Meanwhile, heat a large saucepan with 1 to 2 tablespoons of water. Once hot, scatter in a handful of spinach and as it begins to wilt, add a second handful, continuing this process until all of the spinach is cooked. Season with salt and pepper before draining and pressing and releasing any excess water left in the leaves.

Preheat the grill.

Cut the sausages into bite-sized chunks and return them to the pan with the onion. Add the spinach and pour in half of the sauce, stirring it amongst the leaves.

Pour the remaining sauce on top, followed by the slices of Gruyère cheese. Glaze in the frying pan beneath the grill until golden brown.

more
- *Thickly sliced mushrooms can be fried with the onions.*

serves four

1 tablespoon olive oil
450g (1lb) Cumberland sausages
2 onions, sliced
150ml (5fl oz) single cream
50g (2oz) crème fraîche
75g (3oz) Cheddar cheese, grated
50g (2oz) mozzarella, grated
milk, to loosen
sea salt and pepper
800g (1¾lb) spinach, stalks removed and washed
3–4 slices of Gruyère cheese

seared calves' liver with caramelized grapes and creamy potatoes

These caramelized grapes have a double strength. If you serve them hot, their flavour is sweet and piquant and the full depth of the grape is retained. Cold, they become almost like pickled raisins and taste very good with pâtés. The liver can be two thin slices or one thicker, steak-like cut and is best served with runner beans (see below), French beans or spinach.

To cook the grapes, heat a large frying pan with the ground nut oil. Add the grapes and pan-fry over a medium heat for 8 to 10 minutes until a rich golden brown. Add the butter and soft brown sugar and cook until the sugar dissolves and begins to caramelize. Pour in the brandy and simmer until almost completely evaporated. Follow with the sherry vinegar, boiling until just half the liquid is left, and then the balsamic vinegar. Pour in the sweet white wine and simmer to a syrupy, sauce-like consistency. Season with salt and pepper and leave to infuse.

To cook the liver, heat a frying pan with the vegetable oil and butter. Add the liver and if it's thin slices, cook for just 2 minutes on each side and for steaks, 3 to 4 minutes, leaving a moist, pink centre. Season with salt and pepper.

Serve the liver with the caramelized grapes spooned over the top and creamy mashed potatoes on the side.

more
- *Chopped parsley or chives can be sprinkled over the dish.*
- *If you wish to serve this with runner beans, simply shred the flat runner beans thinly at an angle. Blanch in boiling salted water for a few minutes until just tender, drain and return to the pan with a large knob of butter. Season with a generous twist of pepper and a pinch of sea salt.*

serves four

1 tablespoon vegetable oil
a knob of butter
4 x 175g (6oz) calves' liver steaks or 8 x 75g (3oz) thin slices of calves' liver
salt and pepper
1 x mashed potatoes (see page 142)

for the caramelized grapes
1 tablespoon vegetable or ground nut oil
450g (1lb) white seedless grapes
a small knob of butter
2 heaped teaspoons light soft brown sugar
2 tablespoons brandy
2 tablespoons sherry vinegar
a few drops of balsamic vinegar
150ml (5fl oz) sweet white wine
salt and pepper

slow cooking – one pot
recipes to leave for hours

slow cooking –
one pot recipes to leave for hours

One pot cooking may not be fast, in fact nothing says 'slow cooking' more to me than a simmering pot of meat and vegetables, but this certainly doesn't mean you need to toil away for hours in the kitchen. The beauty of one pot cooking is the swiftness of the preparation and, of course, the lack of washing up! My braised shoulder of lamb with rosemary, honey, carrots and onions may require 4 hours to cook, but it is your oven doing all the work, not you. All you're needed for is to brown the meat, chop a few onions and carrots and add it all to the pot with stock, honey, lemon and herbs.

Real slow cooking is more than just a change of pace. It gives you the chance to use ingredients that require a bit more time for their flavours to develop: deeply savoury cuts of meat, root vegetables, beans and punchy herbs like thyme, rosemary and sage. The blade of beef in red wine beef with bacon crunch may not be as sexy as sirloin or fillet, but it's not as pricey either and after 3 to 4 hours' cooking, the meat is soft and rich. Baked chicken legs with Mediterranean vegetables uses the firmer joint rather than the ubiquitous skinless chicken breast, but the intensely flavoured chicken in this summery dish will be a revelation.

Of course, one pot cooking is a real winter favourite. The idea of chunky one pot pork broth with pasta or lamb with beans, onions, tomatoes and tarragon makes one almost wish for the dark nights to draw in. However, don't think that one pot cooking has to all be country stews and peasant-style bean dishes. My potato, leek and gouda gratin and roast halibut with buttery mussels and herbs are both positively spring-like.

If you're having friends for dinner, one pot cooking can be, without a doubt, a tremendous way of relieving all that stress. Put your dish into the oven on a Saturday afternoon and you can enjoy 4 uninterrupted hours before your guests arrive. Time to make a pudding, a starter and to relax in a long, hot bath (ready for a wonderful culinary experince).

coconut rice and peas with butternut squash

Basmati rice is normally used in this recipe, but here it's being made with arborio, leaving a looser and more risotto-like consistency, which suits a vegetarian main course a lot better.

Halve the butternut squash, scoop out the seeds and cut each half into quarters. Cut away the skin and roughly chop.

Melt the knob of butter in a large pan. Add the chopped onion, sprigs of thyme and squash and gently fry in the butter for a few minutes. Pour in 600ml (1 pint) of the vegetable stock, bring to a simmer and cook for 10 minutes before adding the rice, kidney beans, including the juice, and the coconut milk.

Stir and allow to cook gently for 15 to 20 minutes until the rice is tender. During the cooking time, a little extra vegetable stock may need to be added. The finished consistency should match that of a risotto.

Add the defrosted peas and butter, if using. Season with salt and pepper. The butternut rice and peas is ready to serve.

serves four–six

1 butternut squash
a large knob of butter
1 large onion, finely chopped
1–2 sprigs of thyme (optional)
1–1.1 litres (1½–2 pints) vegetable stock (see note on page 8) or water
350g (12oz) arborio rice (or carnaroli or vialone nano)
410g (14½oz) tin of red kidney beans
400ml (14fl oz) tin of coconut milk
175g (6oz) frozen peas, defrosted
50g (2oz) butter (optional)
salt and pepper

roast halibut with buttery mussels and herbs

In this recipe, halibut is roasted on the bone. Halibut can be quite huge, so speak to your fishmonger and have a fish split down the middle, taking just half.

Preheat the oven to 190°C/375°F/gas 5.

To clean the mussels, scrub the shells in cold water, scraping off any barnacles and pulling away the beards. If any mussels are slightly open, a short, sharp tap should make them close, letting you know they are still alive. Any that don't close should be discarded.

Season the halibut with salt and pepper. Pour 50ml (2fl oz) of water in a buttered roasting tray large enough to hold the halibut and mussels. Put the half halibut in the tin, white skin-side up and bake for 20 minutes.

Add the white wine and mussels and continue to bake for a further 5 to 6 minutes or until the mussels have opened. Remove the tray from the oven and carefully transfer the halibut onto a large warm platter and scatter the mussels around. Discard any mussels that haven't opened.

Place the tray over a high heat, bring the liquid to a rapid simmer and whisk in the butter. If a lot of juices have been left in the tin, boil and allow to evaporate and reduce in volume for a richer flavour. Check for seasoning, finish with a squeeze of lemon and the chopped herbs and pour the sauce over the halibut.

more
- *The top skin of the halibut can be peeled away, revealing the white flesh, before pouring the sauce over.*
- *Serve the fish with plenty of steamed new potatoes.*

serves six

1.5kg (3¼ lb) mussels
2kg (4½lb) half halibut on the bone
sea salt and pepper
1 glass of white wine
75g (3oz) butter
a squeeze of lemon juice
1 heaped tablespoon chopped chives
1 heaped tablespoon chopped chervil
1 heaped tablespoon chopped tarragon
1 heaped tablespoon chopped flat-leaf parsley

baked chicken legs with mediterranean vegetables

The chicken legs are baked with garlic, red onion, aubergine, peppers and courgettes and with the addition of the passata, the dish becomes quite a rustic meal. Crusty bread for dipping and mopping up the juices is highly recommended.

Preheat the oven to 200°C/400°F/gas 6.

Season the chicken legs with salt and pepper. Heat a roasting tray on top of the stove with a drop of olive oil, add the legs and colour to a golden brown. Turn the legs over, add the garlic cloves and roast in the oven for 15 minutes.

Add the red onion, red and yellow peppers and the aubergine. Season with salt and pepper and roast with the chicken for a further 30 minutes until nearly tender.

Add the courgette and return to the oven for a further 10 to 15 minutes until tender. Remove the roasting tray from the oven. The chicken legs should be very moist and tender.

Season the vegetables with salt and pepper, stir in the passata, put on top of the heat and bring to a simmer. Recheck for seasoning and tear the basil leaves, sprinkling them over the chicken and vegetables. The dish is now ready to serve.

serves six

6 chicken legs
salt and pepper
olive oil, for cooking
6 cloves of garlic, not peeled
2 red onions, chopped
2 red peppers, roughly chopped
2 yellow peppers, roughly chopped
1 large aubergine, roughly chopped
4 courgettes, roughly chopped
300ml (10fl oz) passata
a handful of basil leaves

chunky one pot pork broth with pasta

Shoulder or leg of pork suits this recipe, cut into very large chunks to give two to three pieces per person. The meat is slowly simmered with vegetables in the oven and the addition of pasta completes the dish.

Preheat the oven to 150°C/300°F/gas 2.

Put the pork, onion, carrot, leek (if using), bay leaves and thyme in a very large braising pot, pouring the chicken stock over and topping with water to cover the pork. Season with a pinch of salt and pepper and bring to a simmer before covering with a lid and cooking in the oven for 2 to 2½ hours until the meat is completely tender.

Once at this point, cook the pasta in boiling salted water following the packet cooking time. If cooking fresh pasta, simply cook until tender but leaving the slightest of bites.

Once drained, the penne can be added to the pork. Check the seasoning before finishing with the knob of butter and chopped parsley, if using. Ladle the broth into bowls or on plates.

more
- *The cooking liquid has been kept thin to provide the broth. For extra strength, the liquid can be boiled and reduced in volume to increase the flavour. Alternatively, 4 to 5 deseeded and chopped tomatoes can be added at the beginning. As the tomatoes cook, they become pulpy and slightly thicken the stock.*

serves six

2kg (4½lb) shoulder or leg of pork, divided into large chunks (see left)
3 onions, quartered
12 small to medium or 6 large halved carrots, peeled
2 leeks, cut into 5cm (2 inch) pieces (optional)
2 bay leaves
2 sprigs of thyme or sage
1 litre (1¾ pints) chicken stock (see note on page 8)
salt and pepper
225g (8oz) penne pasta
a knob of butter
1 heaped tablespoon coarsely chopped parsley (optional)

braised shoulder of lamb with rosemary, honey, carrots and onions

Preheat the oven to 150°C/300°F/gas 2.

Heat a deep braising pot on top of the stove with 2 to 3 tablespoons of vegetable oil. Season the shoulder with salt and pepper and fry in the pot until well coloured all over. Remove the joint from the pot, absorbing any fat left in the pot with kitchen paper.

Put the carrots and onion quarters in the pot with the sprigs of rosemary, top with the lamb and pour in the stock or water. Bring to a simmer, top with a lid and braise in the oven for 3½ to 4 hours. During the cooking time, the lamb can be turned once or twice to ensure even cooking. Once cooked, remove the shoulder from the pot and keep warm to one side. Pour the cooking liquor into another pan, whisking the butter in, if using.

Meanwhile, heat the braising pot on top of the stove and, once sizzling, add the honey, lemon and rosemary spikes to the vegetables, rolling them in the honey until they become glossy and sticky.

Spoon the carrots and onion quarters onto plates and carve the lamb into thick, steak-like portions, drizzling with the lamb gravy.

more
• If you insist on potatoes, there's mash on page 142.

serves four–six

vegetable oil, for cooking
2kg (4½lb) shoulder of lamb, boned and rolled
salt and pepper
2–3 whole peeled carrots per person
3 onions, peeled and quartered
2 sprigs of rosemary, plus 2 teaspoons rosemary 'spikes'
1 litre (1¾ pints) chicken or lamb stock (see note on page 8) or water
50g (2oz) butter (optional)
2 tablespoons honey
juice of 1 lemon

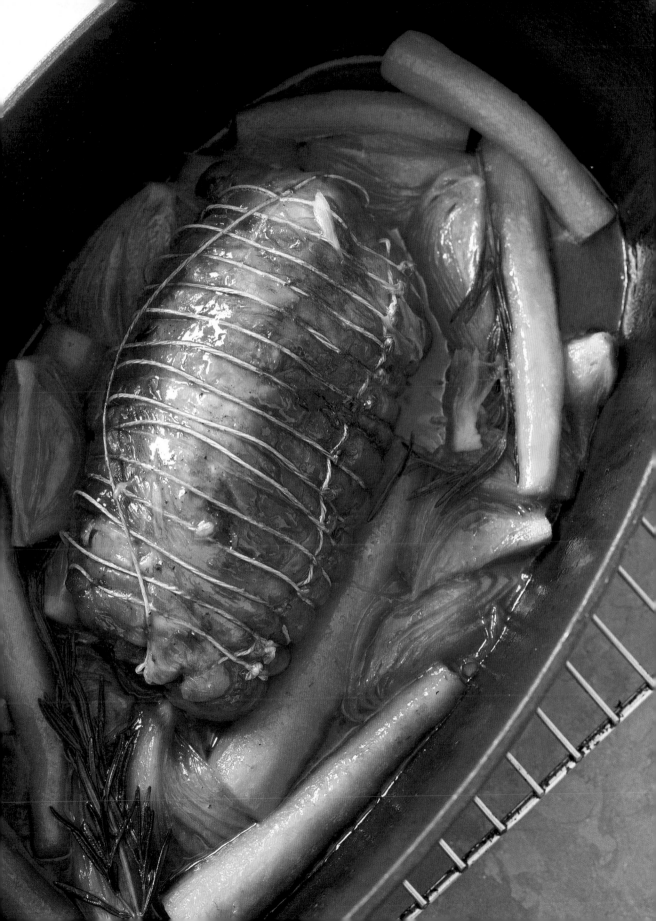

braised rabbit with apples and almonds

Preheat the oven to 160°C/325°F/gas 3.

Season the rabbit legs with salt and pepper and lightly dust each with flour. Heat the oil in a braising pot, adding the rabbit legs and frying to a golden brown.

Remove the legs, wiping the pan of excess fat with kitchen paper before sprinkling in the onions with the cider and honey. Bring to the boil and reduce until there is just a quarter of the cider left. Pour in the apple juice and boil until just half the liquid is left. Return the legs to the pan and pour in the chicken stock, adding water to cover the rabbit, if needed. Bring to a simmer, cover with a lid and braise in the oven for 50 minutes.

While braising the rabbit, peel and core the apples, dividing each into six to eight wedges. Squeeze lemon juice over the pieces to prevent them from discolouring. Add the apple wedges to the pot and continue to simmer for a further 5 to 10 minutes.

Remove the pot from the oven, spooning the rabbit legs, onions and apple into a dish and keeping warm. Boil the cooking liquid to strengthen its flavour, evaporating and reducing in volume until you have about 300ml (10fl oz) liquid left.

Pour in the double cream and simmer for a further 5 to 10 minutes before replacing the rabbit, onions and apple.

Check for seasoning and stir in the almonds and chervil, if using. The rabbit is now ready to serve.

more

- *This creamy, nutty rabbit dish is a great partner for buttered tagliatelle or mashed potatoes. Simple boiled or steamed broccoli is also a good accompaniment.*

serves six

6 large rabbit legs
salt and pepper
flour, for dusting
2 tablespoons vegetable oil
18–24 button onions, peeled
300ml (10fl oz) cider
1 teaspoon honey
300ml (10fl oz) apple juice
600ml (1 pint) chicken stock
  (see note on page 8)
3 apples
a squeeze of lemon juice
150ml (5fl oz) double cream
2 heaped tablespoons flaked
  almonds
1 tablespoon picked chervil
  (optional)

lamb with beans, onions, tomatoes and tarragon

Preheat the oven to 160°C/325°F/gas 3.

Season the lamb neck chunks with sea salt and a twist of pepper and dust with the flour. Heat 2 to 3 tablespoons of the olive oil in a large braising pot and add the lamb, frying and colouring well on all sides. Add the onion and garlic and continue to fry until they begin to soften.

Stir in the tomatoes, red wine, or water if not using, the tinned tomatoes (including all the juices), the haricot beans, the chicken stock cube, 2 sprigs of the tarragon and about 300ml (10fl oz) water to just cover the meat.

Bring to a simmer, cover with a lid and place in the oven, braising slowly for 2½ hours until tender.

Once cooked, transfer the pot on to the stove, remove the lid and skim any excess fat from the top. Should the sauce be too thin, simply bring to a rapid simmer and cook until the liquid has reduced in volume to a thicker consistency and stronger flavour.

Chop the remaining tarragon leaves, add to the pot and check for seasoning. The one pot lamb is now ready to serve as a complete meal.

serves four–six

900g (2lb) lamb neck fillets, cut into large chunks (2–3 per person)
sea salt and pepper
1 heaped tablespoon flour
olive oil, for cooking
3 onions, sliced
4 cloves of garlic, chopped
450g (1lb) tomatoes, quartered and cut into chunks
½ bottle of red wine or 300ml (10fl oz) water
400g (14oz) tin of tomatoes
2 x 400g (14oz) tins of haricot beans, drained and rinsed
1 chicken stock cube (see note on page 8)
4 generous sprigs of tarragon

potato, leek and gouda gratin

In between the layers of potato and leek are slices of Gouda cheese, which enrich the whole dish. Truffle Gouda can also be used. It's very expensive, but it does take the dish up to a different level. A deep 20cm (8 inch) round ovenproof dish is needed to take on all of the ingredients.

Preheat the oven to 180°C/350°F/gas 4.

Heat the butter in a large frying pan. Once bubbling, add the onion and leek and cook, without colouring, for 7 to 8 minutes until beginning to soften. Season with salt and pepper.

Brush the base of a deep 20cm (8 inch) gratin dish with butter. Slice the potatoes thinly on a mandolin and scatter over a layer of potato to cover. Season with salt and pepper and spoon a few dollops of leek and onion on top along with some Gouda. Continue the layers, finishing with a top layer of potatoes. Pour the stock over the top and cover with aluminium foil.

Bake for 45 minutes before removing the foil, brushing the top with butter and continuing to bake for 20 minutes until golden brown. The gratin is best left to stand for 10 minutes, allowing any extra stock to be absorbed by the potatoes.

more
• *Chopped sage can be added to the softened leeks.*

serves three–four as a
    main course or at least
    six as a side dish

50g (2oz) butter, plus extra for brushing
1 large onion, sliced
450g (1lb) leeks, white part only, sliced 5mm (¼ inch) thick
salt and pepper
6 large waxy potatoes, peeled
300g (10oz) Gouda cheese, sliced or grated
300ml (10fl oz) warm vegetable stock (see note on page 8)

red wine beef with bacon crunch

Preheat the oven to 160°C/325°F/gas 3.

Season the beef and dust with flour. Heat 2 tablespoons of oil in a large braising pot. Once hot, colour the beef on all sides before removing from the pot.

Dab away the majority of oil left in the pot with kitchen paper, leaving just a trickle. Add the onions and fry gently until golden brown. Increase the heat and add the mushrooms, stirring once or twice before pouring in the wine with the sugar. Bring to the boil and allow to evaporate until just half the liquid is left.

Put the meat back in the pot, pour in the consommé and top up with 400ml (14fl oz) water. Return to a simmer and add the bay leaves and thyme. Cover with a lid and braise for 2 hours before turning the joint. Return to the oven and continue to braise for a further 1½ hours.

Meanwhile, put the bacon on a baking tray and top with another tray. Place in the oven while braising the beef, checking after 10 minutes. If not deep brown and crispy, continue to bake. Once cooked, transfer to a wire rack.

Once the beef is cooked, remove the joint, onions and mushrooms from the pot and keep warm to one side, skimming off any excess fat from the gravy. Strain the gravy and reboil, reducing by a third in volume for a rich, beefy, red-wine flavour. If a thicker consistency is preferred, thicken with the cornflour, whisking a little at a time into the sauce. Season with salt and pepper.

Slice or break the meat into chunky pieces and return to the sauce with the onions and mushrooms. Serve with the bacon sitting on top and sprinkled with the parsley.

serves six

2kg (4½lb) feather blade of beef, divided into 2 pieces
salt and pepper
flour, for dusting
vegetable oil, for cooking
450g (1lb) button onions
600g (1lb 5oz) button mushrooms
1 bottle of red wine
2 tablespoons soft brown or demerara sugar
2 x 400ml (14fl oz) tins of beef consommé or stock (see note on page 8)
2 bay leaves
2 sprigs of thyme
12 rashers of streaky bacon
1½ teaspoons cornflour (optional), loosened with a little water
a handful of roughly chopped curly parsley (optional)

cooking for pleasure –
when time doesn't matter

cooking for pleasure – when time doesn't matter

There's no stopwatch here, no rush, just the time to enjoy preparing and cooking food. Of course, life is busy, but food shouldn't just be about fast fuel any more than it ought to be about slaving away joylessly over some fiddly recipe. There's so much to discover in slowing things down, choosing fresh ingredients from the market, daring to try something new and cooking for your family and friends with passion.

When I am cooking for pleasure, there are a few things I always find myself doing. Firstly, with a bit more time to think, I put seasonality to the front of my mind. When you're in a rush, it's easy to find yourself, shopping list in hand, throwing expensive air-freighted asparagus, lamb, fish or cherries into your basket as you attempt to follow some summery recipe in darkest November.

Secondly, even when time doesn't matter, I don't really want to spend all day in my kitchen. Of course these recipes are a bit more involved than my 15-minute quick fixes, but many of them are surprisingly simple. The duck confit, marmalade sauté potatoes and orange salad and the aubergine caviar pasta with wilted rocket and parmesan shavings both take an hour or two to cook, and the results are striking, but I find I can have all the prep whizzed through in 20 minutes.

Lastly, if I am cooking for pleasure, it's almost always to share that pleasure with others. That doesn't have to mean a big party, it can just be making something comforting and satisfying for my family at the weekend. The slow-roast belly of pork with melting gorgonzola and apple cabbage is the kind of dish that fits the bill, with its tender meat, crunchy crackling and melting Gorgonzola amongst the cabbage.

If you are having a party (and why not) then my vegetarian ploughman's platter would be a perfect celebratory summer lunch, feeding up to eight people if you prepare all the elements. There are so many more recipes within this chapter to impress your friends with: lamb 'osso buco' or the monkfish with sweet golden sultanas, onion and spinach are a particular couple of my favourites.

vegetarian ploughman's platter

The complete platter requires quite a bit of work to experience all the flavours together. However, each component can also be enjoyed on its own or simply select the few you prefer. The dishes included are a leek and Gruyère cheese quiche, whipped Stilton with figs and watercress (featured on page 51), Italian bruschetta, a natural carrot and orange soup, a green herb salad and a selection of sticks and dips. The platter serves six to eight people.

leek and gruyère quiche

Preheat the oven to 200°C/400°F/gas 6 and butter a 20cm (8 inch) loose-bottomed tart tin.

Heat the butter and olive oil together in a large frying pan. Once sizzling, fry the sliced onion for 5 to 6 minutes before adding the leek. Continue to fry for a further minute or two, then spread them on to a tray to cool.

Break the eggs into a bowl and beat them together with the extra egg yolk, and then add the cream or milk. Stir in the grated cheese and onion and leek and season with the salt and a pinch of cayenne pepper.

Roll out the pastry on a lightly floured surface and line the tart tin, leaving any excess pastry overhanging above the top. Line the pastry case with greaseproof paper and fill with baking beans or dried rice and refrigerate for 20 minutes. Bake blind for 15 to 20 minutes, and then allow to cool. Remove the greaseproof paper and baking beans and cut away the excess pastry. Lower the oven temperature to 160°C/325°F/gas 3.

Pour the filling mixture into the pastry case and bake in the oven for 35 to 40 minutes until just set. Remove the quiche from the oven and leave to rest for 20 minutes before serving just warm.

a large knob of butter
1 tablespoon olive oil
1 large onion, sliced
1 large/medium leek, finely shredded and washed
2 eggs
1 egg yolk
150ml (5fl oz) double cream or milk
100g (4oz) Gruyère cheese, grated
salt
a pinch of cayenne pepper
175g (6oz) fresh or frozen ready-made shortcrust pastry

whipped stilton with figs and watercress (recipe on page 51)

italian bruschetta

Brush the bread slices with olive oil and toast on both sides. Once toasted, the bread can be rubbed with the garlic.

Halve and deseed the tomatoes, cutting each into roughly 1cm (½ inch) cubes. Mix the tomatoes and mozzarella in a bowl, season with salt and pepper and drizzle with the olive oil. Tear the basil leaves over the bruschetta, adding a few dots of balsamic vinegar, if using. Spoon on top of the garlic toasts and serve.

6 thick slices of French bread or ciabatta
olive oil, for drizzling
1 clove of garlic, peeled and halved
3 plum tomatoes
1–2 buffalo mozzarella, chopped, or broken into nuggets
sea salt and pepper
a handful of basil leaves
balsamic vinegar (optional)

natural carrot and orange soup

In a saucepan, simmer all of the ingredients together for about 20 minutes until the carrots have softened. Pour into a blender and blend until totally smooth. If too thick, simply loosen with water. The soup can be eaten hot or cold and served in tea cups.

450g (1lb) carrots, peeled and roughly chopped
600ml (1 pint) carrot juice (if unavailable, replace with water or vegetable stock) (see note on page 8)
300ml (10fl oz) fresh orange juice

more
• The soup can be blitzed with a handheld blender for a lighter, frothy finish.

green herb salad

Mix together the mustard, salt, sugar and vinegar and whisk the oil in slowly. This dressing keeps well in a screw-top jar.

Mix together the salad leaves and herbs, drizzling with the dressing when ready to serve.

1 bag of mixed salad leaves (a few handfuls)
1–2 handfuls of herb sprigs (chervil, basil, flat-leaf parsley, tarragon, chive sticks)

for the dressing
1 teaspoon Dijon mustard
a pinch of salt
a pinch of sugar
1 tablespoon red or white wine vinegar
75ml (3fl oz) olive oil

sticks and dips

Choose from the following selection of vegetables, cutting each into sticks. Not all of the dips need to be offered, one or two is plenty.

for the sticks
carrots / cucumber / asparagus spears / sweet peppers / spring onions
Cut the chosen vegetables into sticks.

for the cocktail sauce dip
2–3 tablespoons tomato ketchup / 150g (5oz) mayonnaise / 1–2 splashes of brandy / salt and pepper
Whisk the ketchup into the mayonnaise and stir in the brandy to help balance the strong tomato taste. Season with salt and pepper if needed.

more
• A squeeze of lemon juice can be stirred in. A few tablespoons of crème fraîche or natural yoghurt are also an option for a creamier sauce.

for the aïoli sauce
2 small cloves of garlic / salt and pepper / 1 teaspoon Dijon mustard / 1 tablespoon lemon juice or white wine vinegar / 150g (5 oz) mayonnaise
Crush the garlic cloves, adding a generous pinch of salt once all smashed. Now, using the tip of a large knife, crush the garlic a stage further to a smooth pulp.

Put the garlic, mayonnaise, mustard and lemon juice into a bowl, whisking all together. Season with salt and pepper. If too thick, loosen with 1 to 2 tablespoons water.

more
• This recipe can easily be halved in volume, using just 1 large clove of garlic.

for the wholegrain mustard dip
100g (4oz) mayonnaise / 50g (2oz) crème fraîche / 1 tablespoon wholegrain mustard / 1 teaspoon honey, optional
Whisk all of the above together.

chard and mushroom pies

Boil a saucepan of salted water. Add the washed chard and cook for several minutes until tender. Plunge into a bowl of iced water to refresh before draining and squeezing to release any excess water.

Melt the butter in a frying pan. Once sizzling, add the shallot and fry until just softening. Stir in the mushroom, seasoning with salt, pepper and a squeeze of lemon juice, if using. Cook over a medium to high heat until the mushroom juices have evaporated and the mixture is fairly dry. Leave to cool before mixing with the chard and seasoning.

Preheat the oven to 200°C/400°F/gas 6.

Unroll the pastry, dividing one of the sheets into four rectangles and placing them on a baking tray lined with parchment paper. Prick the base of each one with a fork. Spoon the chard and mushroom mix on to the pastry bases, leaving a 1–1.5cm (½–⅝ inch) border. Mix together the egg yolk and milk and brush it around the borders.

Cut the remaining sheet of pastry in four, rolling out each on a lightly floured surface until large enough to cover the pies. Place the pastry on top of the chard, pressing firmly around the border to seal.

Refrigerate the pies for 20 minutes to firm up before trimming the edges for a neat finish. Brush each pastry with the remaining egg yolk mix and bake for 20 to 25 minutes until well coloured and crispy.

Meanwhile, to make the mushroom sauce, place the shallot and mushroom in a saucepan Add the stock and cream with the wine, if using. Bring to the boil and then simmer for 10 minutes, adding a squeeze of lemon juice and seasoning. Pour the sauce into a blender and blend until smooth, then strain through a fine sieve. Serve the hot pies with the mushroom sauce poured over.

serves four

450g (1lb) chard leaves
1 tablespoon butter
225g (8oz) shallots, peeled and sliced
450g (1lb) mushrooms, sliced (if cultivated)
salt and pepper
a squeeze of lemon juice (optional)
2 x 375g (13oz) packets of ready-rolled puff pastry
1 egg yolk
1 tablespoon milk

for the mushroom cream sauce
1 shallot, peeled and chopped
100g (4oz) button mushrooms, sliced
150ml (5fl oz) vegetable stock (see note on page 8)
150ml (5fl oz) double cream
a splash of white wine (optional)
a squeeze of lemon juice
salt and pepper

baked ratatouille peppers with melting goat's cheese

These peppers may look rustic, but the beauty here is in eating them, particularly when accompanied by a slice of focaccia bread and a tossed salad.

Preheat the oven to 160°C/325°F/gas 3.

Halve the peppers lengthways, removing the seeds but leaving the stalks intact. Season and place on a greased baking tray.

Heat the olive oil in a large frying pan and add the chopped aubergine, courgette, onion and garlic. Fry over a medium heat for 5 to 6 minutes until just beginning to soften. Season with salt and pepper.

Stir the tomatoes into the vegetables and divide the ratatouille into the peppers. Bake in the oven for 50 to 60 minutes until the sweet peppers are tender.

Once cooked, top each of the peppers with the goat's cheese and increase the oven temperature to 190°C/375°F/gas 5. Cook for a further 5 to 6 minutes until the goat's cheese has melted. Divide among plates or bowls, drizzling with any juices left in the tray..

serves four

4 red peppers
sea salt and pepper
4 tablespoons olive oil
1 medium aubergine, cut into large cubes
2 courgettes, cut into large cubes
1 large onion, chopped
2 large cloves of garlic, chopped
4 plum tomatoes, roughly chopped
8 thick slices of goat's cheese

aubergine caviar pasta with wilted rocket and parmesan shavings

This takes a bit of time, but involves so little work. The sauce is basically just home-made aubergine caviar loosened with crème fraîche and vegetable stock from a carton or made using a stock cube. The best pastas to use are penne, macaroni or that long hollow spaghetti, bucatini.

Preheat the oven to 200°C/400°F/gas 6.

To make the caviar, cut the aubergines in half lengthways and score the flesh in a criss-cross fashion. Insert the garlic slices into the cuts and season with sea salt.

Put the aubergines, cut-side up, on a large sheet of foil on a baking tray and drizzle with olive oil. Wrap the foil to seal and bake in the oven for 20 minutes before reducing the oven temperature to 150°C/300°F/gas 2 and continuing to bake for a further 50 minutes until completely softened.

Unwrap the aubergines, scraping the flesh from the skin into a blender or food processor. Blend until completely smooth and transfer to a saucepan. Warm and whisk in 150g (5oz) of the crème fraîche, adding the remaining amount for a creamier finish. To loosen to a thick but pouring consistency, stir in some vegetable stock, a little at a time, until the sauce stage is reached. Season with salt and pepper.

Cook the pasta in boiling salted water until tender but leaving a slight bite, before draining.

Add the aubergine caviar sauce to the pasta, bring to a simmer and stir in the rocket leaves. Season with salt and pepper and, using a potato peeler, finish with shavings of Parmesan and a trickle of olive oil.

serves four

for the aubergine caviar
2 large aubergines
2 cloves of garlic, sliced
sea salt and pepper
olive oil, for drizzling
150–250g (5–9oz) crème fraîche
vegetable stock, to loosen (see left) (see note on page 8)

400g (14oz) pasta (see left)
a handful or two of rocket leaves
sea salt and pepper
Parmesan cheese, for shaving
extra-virgin olive oil, for sprinkling

slow-roast belly of pork with melting gorgonzola and apple cabbage

Although it needs 3 hours slow roasting, the beauty of this cut of pork is that it looks after itself. As the fat content melts it bastes the meat, leaving the most succulent of joints, so soft it carves with a spoon.

Preheat the oven to 160°C/325°F/gas 3.

Season the meat side of the pork belly with salt and pepper and place the joint, skin-side up, on a wire rack over a roasting tray. Brush the skin with oil, sprinkle liberally with sea salt and roast in the oven for 3 hours before removing and leaving to rest.

While roasting the pork, cut the cabbage into six wedges, discarding any coarse outside leaves and the central white core. Each wedge can now be finely shredded.

Finely slice four of the shallots, placing all of the remaining ones in a saucepan with the chicken stock and sugar. About 20 to 30 minutes before the pork finishes cooking, bring the stock to a simmer and poach the shallots until soft and the cooking liquid has reduced to become sticky, leaving a nice shiny glaze over the shallots. Season.

While the pork is resting, cook the cabbage in boiling salted water for a few minutes until tender and drain in a colander. Melt the butter in a saucepan and add the finely sliced shallots, cooking over a medium heat until they begin to soften. Add the apple, cooking for a further minute before stirring in the cabbage and seasoning. The Gorgonzola pieces can now be stirred into the cabbage, melting as they warm.

Cut the crackling from the belly, snapping it into large pieces. Carve the pork in thick slices, dividing it among the plates along with a spoonful of the cabbage and the shallots.

serves four

1kg (2¼lb) belly of pork, skin scored
sea salt and pepper
vegetable oil, for brushing
1 small savoy cabbage
20 shallots, peeled
300ml (½ pint) chicken stock (see note on page 8)
a pinch of demerara or light soft brown sugar
25g (1oz) butter
2 apples, grated
100g (4oz) room-temperature Gorgonzola, broken into pieces

warm lobster, new potato and mixed leaf salad with lobster dressing and pistachio butter

For the lobster dressing, a few spoons of tinned lobster bisque are added. This is not essential, but does add another strength, enhancing the warm lobster.

Cook the new potatoes in boiling salted water for 20 minutes or until tender before draining and keeping warm.

Meanwhile, shell the lobster tails, splitting each in half. Crack the claws with the back of a heavy knife and remove the meat and nuggets, leaving the claws whole.

Whisk together the olive oil, white wine vinegar and lobster bisque, to taste, seasoning with salt and pepper.

Mix together the butter and chopped pistachio nuts (these can be blended in a small food processor) to create a green pistachio butter.

You can serve the lobsters cold or warm in a few tablespoons of water, adding the large knob of butter and seasoning with salt and pepper. It's important that the stove is on a low heat and the lobsters covered with a lid and warmed for just a few minutes.

Slice the new potatoes into three to four pieces each and divide among four plates or bowls. Place a small handful of lettuce on top of each. Warm the lobster dressing before pouring 2 to 3 tablespoons over the potatoes and lettuce leaves. Present the lobster claws, trimmings and tail on top of the lettuce and finish with a dollop of pistachio butter, melting over the lobster.

serves four

8–12 new potatoes
2 x 750g (1lb 10oz) cooked
    lobsters
50ml (2fl oz) olive oil
2 teaspoons white wine
    vinegar or lemon juice
3–4 tablespoons tinned
    lobster bisque
salt and pepper
100g (4oz) butter, plus 1 large
    knob
25g (1oz) shelled pistachios,
    finely chopped
a few handfuls (or 1 bag) of
    mixed salad leaves

monkfish with sweet golden sultanas, onion and spinach

Pan-fry the sliced onion in a little of the olive oil over a medium heat until softened. Increase the heat and continue to fry until a caramel golden brown.

Meanwhile, put the golden sultanas in a saucepan and top with the sweet white wine. Bring to a simmer, allowing the wine to evaporate until it is a thick syrupy consistency. Mix the sultanas with the fried onion.

While cooking the onion and sultanas, the herb butter sauce can be made. Boil together the white wine vinegar and 1 tablespoon of the lemon juice until just half the liquid is left. Add the double cream and, once simmering, whisk in the butter, a little at a time. Season with salt and ground white pepper, loosening, if necessary, with the extra lemon juice or water. Keep warm to one side.

Heat 2 tablespoons of the olive oil in a frying pan. Season the monkfish fillets with salt and pepper, place them in the pan and sear in the hot oil, turning to brown evenly. Once coloured, cook for 3 to 4 minutes on each side until just firm, but with a light spring left when you touch them.

Meanwhile, melt the knob of butter in a large pan over a high heat. Add the spinach leaves, seasoning with salt and pepper, and stir the leaves until wilted and tender, before draining in a colander.

Divide the spinach and golden sultana onions among four plates, topping the onions with the monkfish. Add the chopped herbs to the butter sauce, pour around and serve.

serves four

2 onions, thinly sliced
olive oil, for cooking
4 heaped tablespoons golden sultanas
200ml (7fl oz) sweet white wine
4 x 150–175g (5–6oz) monkfish fillets
salt and pepper
a knob of butter
600g (1lb 5oz) spinach, stalks removed and washed
2 anchovy fillets, chopped (optional)

for the herb butter sauce
1 tablespoon white wine vinegar
1–2 tablespoons lemon juice
2 tablespoons double cream
100g (4oz) cold unsalted butter, diced
salt and ground white pepper
1 heaped tablespoon mixed herbs (chives, tarragon, chervil, parsley)

duck confit, marmalade sauté potatoes and orange salad

The duck takes up to 2 hours to cook, barely simmering in the duck fat or oil, but can also be cooked several days or weeks in advance. Keep the legs totally immersed in the fat and refrigerated until needed.

Preheat the oven to 150°C/300°F/gas 2.

Lightly salt the duck legs. Warm the fat in a roasting tray or saucepan, place the ducks in the tray and bring to a very gentle simmer. Cover with foil or a lid and cook in the oven for 2 hours until the legs are completely tender. Once cooked, leave the legs to relax in the fat for 15 minutes before lifting out and pan-frying, skin-side down, to a rich, crispy, golden brown. Sprinkle lightly with sea salt before serving.

Meanwhile, cook the new potatoes in boiling salted water for 20 minutes until tender. Drain and halve the potatoes, pan-frying in some of the duck fat to a golden brown colour. Add the sliced onions (these can also be fried separately) and continue to fry until softened and golden brown. Season with salt and pepper and stir in the marmalade.

Top and tail the oranges. The rind and pith can now be removed by cutting in a sawing motion down the sides. To release the segments, cut between each membrane, saving all the juice.

Mix together the orange segments and salad leaves. Whisk together a couple of tablespoons of saved orange juice and the oil, seasoning with salt and pepper, and drizzle the dressing over the leaves. Serve the salad with the warm duck and potatoes.

serves six

for the confit
6 duck legs
sea salt
900ml (1½ pints) melted duck fat or pork fat (lard)

for the potatoes
750g (1½lb) new potatoes
2 large onions, sliced
salt and pepper
2 heaped tablespoons orange marmalade

for the salad
3 oranges
200g (7oz) mixed or a single variety of salad leaves (rocket, curly endive, little gems, watercress)
2–3 tablespoons olive or walnut oil
salt and pepper

roast rack of pork with turnip and prune dauphinois

It's best to ask for the pork to be French trimmed, as per a rack of lamb. Also, if possible, have the chine bone removed so you can cut between each rib with ease.

Preheat the oven to 190°C/375°F/gas 5.

Cover the rack bones with foil to prevent them from burning and season the underside of the rack with salt and pepper. Place in a roasting tray and brush with the oil, seasoning the skin with table salt and a sprinkling of coarse sea salt.

Before roasting the pork, rub a large, deep ovenproof dish with the garlic, brushing with half the butter and seasoning with salt and white pepper. Mix the sliced turnip with the cream, also seasoning, before layering half of them in the dish. Top with an even layer of the prunes and finish with the remaining turnip, leaving it rustic or with a neat finish.

The pork and dauphinois can now be cooked in the oven for 15 to 20 minutes before reducing the temperature to 150°C/300°F/gas 2 and continuing to bake for a further 45 to 50 minutes. At this point, remove the pork rack from the oven and leave to rest. Check the dauphinois and if it is still slightly firm, cook for a further 15 to 20 minutes until it is tender and lightly golden.

While relaxing the pork, drain any excess fat from the roasting tray. Warm over a medium to hot heat, adding the honey. As the honey begins to bubble and sizzle, turning to a light caramel, add the stock and return to a simmer. Cook gently for a few minutes, seasoning if needed. Whisk in the butter, if using, before straining through a fine sieve.

The pork is now ready to serve with a scoop of the turnip and prune dauphinois and a drizzle of the sweet gravy.

serves six–eight

1 rack of pork (6–8 bones),
  French trimmed (see left)
salt and pepper
vegetable oil, for brushing
sea salt, for sprinkling
1 tablespoon honey or
  golden syrup
300ml (10fl oz) chicken stock
  (see note on page 8)
25–50g (1–2oz) butter
  (optional)

*for the turnip and prune
  dauphinois*
1 large clove of garlic,
  peeled and halved
25g (1oz) butter
salt and ground white pepper
1kg (2¼lb) peeled turnips,
  thinly sliced
600ml (1 pint) double cream
  (½ cream and ½ milk can
  also be used)
300g (10oz) ready-to-eat
  prunes

lamb 'osso buco'

Osso buco is an Italian dish made with veal steaks taken from the hind shin of the calf. Translated, it means 'bone with a hole', referring to the hole found inside the circle of meat. It's said that tomatoes should not be included, however I've added them here, their sweetness giving a rich flavour and their flesh becoming a thickening agent. Gremolata is another addition, basically just chopped parsley and garlic and grated lemon zest, all suiting my choice of lamb perfectly. Classically, this osso buco is served with risotto Milanese, to be found here on page 119.

Preheat the oven to 160°C/325°F/gas 3.

Heat a large ovenproof pan (big enough to fit a single layer of the steaks) with the olive oil. Season the lamb with salt and pepper and lightly dust with the flour. Add the steaks and brown well on both sides before removing from the pan.

Add the onion and celery, if using, and cook over a medium heat for 8 to 10 minutes until softening. Add the chopped tomato and return the steaks to the pan, pouring in the wine with the orange juice, zest strips, bay leaf and consommé. Bring to the simmer before covering with a lid or triple layer of aluminium foil. Put the steaks in the pre-heated oven and braise for 1½ to 2 hours until the meat is very tender and almost falling off the bone.

Once the lamb is cooked, remove the meat from the pan, keeping warm to one side. Boil the liquid over a brisk heat, allowing to reduce in volume by 100 to 150ml (3½ to 5fl oz) to strengthen the sauce flavour. The butter, if using, can now be whisked into the sauce for a richer, glossy finish.

Mix together the gremolata ingredients and stir into the sauce, leaving to infuse for a minute before spooning the sauce over the lamb steaks and serving.

serves four

2 tablespoons olive oil
4 x 250–300g (9–10oz) leg of lamb steaks, 2.5cm (1 inch) thick
salt and pepper
2 tablespoons flour
1 large onion, chopped
2 sticks of celery, chopped (optional)
3 plum tomatoes, halved, deseeded and chopped
300ml (10fl oz) white wine
2 strips of orange zest, plus 150ml (5fl oz) fresh orange juice
1 bay leaf
400ml (14fl oz) tin of beef consommé or lamb stock (see note on page 8)
50g (2oz) butter

for the gremolata
2 heaped tablespoons chopped parsley
1 level tablespoon finely grated lemon zest
1 small clove of garlic, finely chopped

quick puddings –
ready in 20 minutes

quick puddings – ready in 20 minutes

Not all the best puddings take hours of hard work, waiting for soufflés to rise and pastry to relax. A bowl of plump raspberries, spoonfuls of thick country cream and some toasted nuts are some of the simpler, natural sweet flavours to enjoy.

If you have fruit in your house, you'll always have pudding. In the winter, bake with a little sugar to intensify the flavour, as I've done with my toasted ginger figs and gently pan-fried Cognac peaches. In the warmer months, with fruit burstingly ripe, you need only cut up to create a simple fruit platter, a very refreshing way to bring a meal to a close. Another booster for the natural flavour of fruit is to steep in alcohol, as you'll find with the liqueur-steeped summer fruits with lemon curd cream.

Chocolate is an essential quick pudding stand-by. Finish a meal with, quite simply, espressos and squares of 70 percent cocoa dark chocolate. The white chocolate cream that I serve with a Caribbean fruit salad can be whipped up in minutes and, pure white, it is an elegant chocolate mousse that could be served with any fruit or biscuits.

I love having a creamy element to my desserts and I've provided lots of ideas in this chapter that could be mixed and matched as you desire. Zabaglione, that frothy Italian dessert, is paired here with chunks of banana and pecan nuts, but is certainly open to all fruit offers. There's also a tiramisu bocker glory where the mascarpone cream provides a perfect accompaniment for coffee and brandy-soaked sponge fingers, but would also be a good match for any chocolate sauce, chocolate shavings or crushed amaretti biscuits.

One thing to remember is that quick puddings don't have to be cold puddings. Sugar, fruit and chocolate take no time at all to warm up or melt so you can easily be tucking into hot cognac peaches with pistachio brioche and jersey cream or chocolate and nut pancakes with maple syrup and extra-thick cream in under 20 minutes.

banana and pecan nut zabaglione

Zabaglione is a classic Italian frothy dessert, usually flavoured with Marsala, but any sweet wine, sherry or fruit-based alcohol can be used.

Place the egg yolks, sugar and alcohol in a large bowl over a pan of gently simmering water. Using a balloon whisk or electric hand whisk, slowly whisk the mix until it becomes light and frothy. Increase the speed and continue to whisk for 8 to 10 minutes until the zabaglione has reached a thick, creamy, whipped meringue stage. Remove the bowl from the pan and keep warm to one side.

Slice or chop the bananas into chunks, sprinkling with a squeeze of lemon juice. Stir in the chopped pecan nuts and divide among glasses or bowls, topping each one with the warm zabaglione.

more
* *Blueberries would go well with the bananas. Mixed summer fruits are another favourite, topped with a raspberry eau-de-vie-flavoured zabaglione*

serves four

4 egg yolks
75g (3oz) caster sugar
100ml (3½fl oz) Marsala or
   sweet sherry
4 bananas
a squeeze of lemon juice
50g (2oz) pecan nuts,
   chopped

tiramisu bocker glory

Beat together the mascarpone and icing sugar until creamy. Lightly whip the cream to a soft peak before folding into the mascarpone.

In a bowl, mix together the cold coffee and brandy. Snap each of the sponge fingers in half, dip eight pieces into the coffee and arrange in four knickerbocker glory glasses or bowls. If using, spoon a little cold chocolate sauce over each.

The mascarpone can now be piped on top using a piping bag. Layer up the sponge fingers, chocolate sauce and mascarpone cream twice more, finishing with the mascarpone cream.

A dusting of cocoa powder or finely grated chocolate can be sprinkled on top, if preferred.

serves four

500g (18oz) mascarpone cheese
4 heaped tablespoons sifted icing sugar
150ml (5fl oz) double cream
150ml (5fl oz) cold espresso coffee
4 tablespoons brandy
12 sponge fingers (savoiardi biscuits)
1 x chocolate sauce (see page 236) (optional)
cocoa powder or finely grated dark chocolate (optional)

mango cheesecake fool

A packet of brandy snaps is quite handy to have in-house when making this pud, ready for dunking into the fool or crumbling over the top.

Peel the mangoes and cut away the flesh from the stone, chopping it roughly once all removed. Liquidize in a blender until smooth.

While blending the mangoes, beat together the cream cheese and caster sugar in a bowl until soft and creamy. In a separate bowl, lightly whip the cream to a soft peak stage.

Stir the mango purée into the cream cheese and fold in the lightly whipped cream. Spoon the cheesecake fool into one large bowl or individual glasses.

more
- *A few wrinkled passion fruits can be halved and scooped out, scattering their rich orange and black dotted pulp over the fool. Passion fruits are quite pungent and powerful in aroma and flavour and so to lessen their sharp bite, simply stir a teaspoon or two of icing sugar into the juicy seeds.*
- *Refrigerating the fool for several hours creates a firmer consistency.*

serves four–six

2 large ripe mangoes
300g (10oz) cream cheese
3 heaped tablespoons
    caster sugar
150ml (5fl oz) double cream

liqueur-steeped summer fruits with lemon curd cream

Raspberries, strawberries, blackberries, blueberries, blackcurrants and redcurrants all suit this recipe; you can choose as many or as few as you wish. The liqueur is best if it is raspberry or strawberry-flavoured, both fruits working so well with the lemon curd cream. The steeping time here is just 15 to 20 minutes, but if you're prepared to wait an hour or two more, it will be even better

Put the fruits in a large bowl. Sprinkle with the sugar and liqueur and leave to steep for 15 to 20 minutes, stirring gently every 5 minutes to ensure all are coated and flavoured.

Whisk together the cream and lemon curd to a soft peak.

The fruits and lemon curd cream are now ready to serve, drizzled with the sweet liqueur syrup.

serves four

450g (1lb) mixed summer berries, hulled (see left)
3 tablespoons caster sugar
3 tablespoons raspberry or strawberry liqueur (crème de framboises or fraises or a fruit-flavoured eau-de-vie)
125ml (4½fl oz) double cream
5 tablespoons lemon curd, chilled

white chocolate cream with caribbean fruit salad

In a small saucepan, bring 100ml (3½fl oz) of the cream to the boil. Add the chocolate, stirring until completely melted. Pour the chocolate cream into a bowl and leave to cool.

Meanwhile, peel the mango, cutting the flesh carefully away from the stone before chopping into chunks. Halve the papaya, scooping out the seeds with a spoon. Divide each half into three wedges, cutting away the skin, then slice each piece into chunks. Chop the pineapple chunks into smaller pieces.

Top and tail the oranges. The rind and pith can now be removed by cutting in a sawing motion down the sides. To release the segments, cut between each membrane. Mix all of the fruits together.

If making the mango sauce, remove the skin from the fruit, cutting away the flesh from the stone before whizzing in a blender with the caster sugar until smooth. Strain through a sieve.

Whip the remaining cream to soft peaks, folding in the cooled chocolate to complete the mousse. If too loose, continue to whisk to a soft peak.

Serve a dollop of the white chocolate cream with a spoonful or two of the fruit salad, drizzling with the mango sauce, if using.

more
- *For a warm spiced mousse, add the seeds from 1 scraped vanilla pod along with a grating of fresh nutmeg to the cream before heating.*
- *Puff pastry palmiers, available in most large stores, are perfect for dipping in the mousse.*

serves four–six

for the white chocolate cream
300ml (10fl oz) double cream
225g (8oz) white chocolate, finely chopped

for the fruit salad
1 large mango
1 large papaya
1 bag (approximately 200–250g/7–9oz) of pre-cut fresh pineapple
1–2 oranges

for the mango sauce (optional)
1 large mango
1 tablespoon caster sugar

french toast gingerbread and pineapple sandwich

Fresh pre-cut pineapple chunks are often very large and should be halved to make them easier to eat.

To make the pineapple, heat a frying pan or wok. Melt the butter in the pan and when beginning to foam, add the pineapple pieces. Fry for a few minutes to warm through before sprinkling over the sugar. Slightly increase the heat and the sugar will begin to caramelize. Stir the pineapple and pour in the lime juice to lift the caramel from the base of the pan, creating a syrup. If it's too thick, loosen with a tablespoon or two of water.

Meanwhile, in a bowl beat together the eggs, cream and sugar and pour it into a tray. Dip the gingerbread slices in the mix just long enough for them to soften. Heat another frying pan with the butter. Once it begins to foam, add the soaked gingerbread slices, and pan-fry gently for 1 to 2 minutes on each side until golden.

Place four slices on four serving plates, spoon over the warm syrupy pineapple chunks and complete the sandwiches with the remaining gingerbread slices.

more
- *Fresh pouring cream would be wonderful to drizzle over.*
- *The lime juice can be replaced with a generous splash of rum.*

serves four

2 eggs
4 tablespoons single cream
2 teaspoons caster sugar
8 slices (approximately 1–1.5cm/½–5/8 inch thick) of gingerbread cake
25g (1oz) butter

for the pineapple
15g (½oz) butter
350g (12oz) pre-cut fresh pineapple chunks
2 tablespoons light soft brown sugar
juice of 1 lime

strawberry eton mess with raspberry sauce

The strawberries, cream and raspberry sauce can also be spooned and drizzled into pavlova meringue cases for a differently styled dessert.

To make the raspberry sauce, place the berries and icing sugar in a blender, quickly blitzing to a purée. Push through a sieve, loosening the smooth sauce with a drop of water if too thick.

Break the meringues into chunky pieces. Roughly chop two thirds of the strawberries, halving the remainder.

Whip the double cream to a soft peak, folding in the chopped strawberries, broken meringues and half of the raspberry sauce to create a ripple effect.

Divide the 'mess' among the bowls, finishing each with the halved strawberries and a drizzle of the remaining raspberry sauce.

more
* A vanilla pod, halved and scraped of seeds, can be added to the cream before whipping for a rich vanilla taste. The pods can then be divided into long thin strips and used as a garnish.

serves four–six

225g (8oz) raspberries
50g (2oz) icing sugar
4 individual meringues
450g (1lb) strawberries, hulled
600ml (1 pint) double cream

cognac peaches with pistachio brioche and jersey cream

Peach schnapps can be used in place of Cognac or totally forget the alcohol and leave the peaches just sweetened. Jersey cream has the richest of flavours, complementing the quite powerful peaches perfectly.

Preheat the grill. Put the brioche slices on a baking tray and toast beneath the grill on one side only, then leave to cool.

Chop the pistachios, mixing them with 50g (2oz) of the softened butter and the icing sugar. Turn the toasted brioche over on the tray and spread each slice with the sweet pistachio butter. Leave to one side.

Halve the peaches, remove the stone and cut each half into three wedges. Heat a large non-stick frying pan on the stove. Add the remaining butter and once it starts to foam, tip the peaches into the pan. Sprinkle with the caster sugar and pan-fry for a few minutes to soften. Pour in the Cognac (once warmed it will ignite, so do be careful), stir just once or twice and the peaches are ready.

Meanwhile, return the brioche slices under the grill and toast to a golden brown. Serve the peaches scooped on to the toasts, drizzling with any juices left in the pan. Finish with the Jersey cream.

serves four

4 thick slices of brioche loaf
1 heaped tablespoon shelled pistachios
75g (3oz) butter, softened
1 heaped tablespoon icing sugar
4 peaches
1 tablespoon caster sugar
2 tablespoons Cognac
Jersey cream, to serve

toasted ginger figs

Four or five fig halves per person are plenty with pouring cream to drizzle over.

Preheat the grill.

Mix the caster sugar and ginger together in a bowl. Press the cut side of the figs in the ginger sugar and place, sugared-side up, on a baking tray. Sprinkle any remaining sugar over the fruits.

Put beneath the grill, not too close to the top, and cook for 6 to 8 minutes until toasted with a tinged edge. Offer a jug of the double cream ready to drizzle over.

serves six

4 tablespoons caster sugar
1 teaspoon ground ginger
12–15 figs, halved
150–300ml (5–10fl oz) double
  cream

chocolate and nut pancakes with maple syrup and extra-thick cream

Sift together the flour and cocoa powder. Melt the butter and whisk in the milk, eggs, sugar and a pinch of salt. Pour into the flour and whisk vigorously before stirring in the chopped pecan nuts.

Heat a frying pan with a trickle of oil. Spoon the batter into the pan, five to six pancakes at a time, and cook over a gentle heat for a few minutes until small bubbles appear on the surface and the pancakes are ready to be turned over. Continue to fry for a further 1 to 2 minutes before removing them from the pan. To keep warm while cooking the remaining pancakes, simply wrap in a warm tea towel.

The pancakes are now ready to offer with the maple syrup and extra-thick cream to be drizzled and dolloped on top.

makes 25–30 pancakes

175g (6oz) self-raising flour
50g (2oz) cocoa powder
25g (1oz) butter
200ml (7fl oz) milk
2 eggs, beaten
100g (4oz) caster sugar
salt
75g (3oz) pecan nuts, chopped
vegetable oil, for frying
maple syrup, to serve
150–300ml (5–10fl oz) extra-thick double cream

proper puddings –
worth every minute

proper puddings –
worth every minute

Sometimes there just isn't a rush is there? I love an extravagant pudding and I would never begrudge a moment spent putting one together. The artistry and precision required are a joy quite unlike any other aspect of cooking.

Certainly, I would make one of these for myself but, really, there is no better time to indulge than when having friends or family round to eat. For so many people the pudding is the highlight of the meal and it's so nice to see the look on your guests' faces when the dessert is presented, one you've taken just that extra little bit of care over.

Puddings do, however, require good timing and one of the best ways to take the pressure off when you're preparing a special meal is to, where possible, make your pudding in advance. That way on the day of the dinner you can concentrate on your main course without your cake clashing with the beef for a spot in the oven or your custard and soup jostling for position on the stoves. The iced jersey cream with lots of strawberries, the passion fruit mousse **with passion fruit jelly and sauce** and the raspberry and white chocolate cream shortbreads are all puddings that can be prepared in advance and ask for no more than a little last minute arranging on the day.

The other thing to take into consideration when choosing your pudding is what you'll be having for the rest of the meal. If the main course is rich and your guests are likely to be quite full, then you'll find they will welcome a refreshing fruit-based pudding like my baked amaretti peaches or blackberry clafoutis. However, I find that if you are having something a little lighter like fish, then why not treat your friends to something with a richer edge, like the hazelnut cake with frangelico cream or the poached nutty meringues.

prune and armagnac bread and butter pudding

Prune and Armagnac ice cream and tart are French classics and here these flavours have been borrowed to introduce into one of our greats.

Preheat the oven to 160°C/325°F/gas 3. Butter a 1.5–1.8 litre (2½–3 pint) pudding dish. Soak the prunes in the Armagnac for several hours or overnight.

Butter the bread. Split the vanilla pod lengthways, if using, and put the pod or extract in a saucepan with the cream and milk and bring to the boil.

While it's heating, whisk together the egg yolks and sugar in a bowl. Once it's at boiling point, whisk the cream into the egg yolks. Allow the cream to cool a little before removing the vanilla pod. Drain the prunes in a sieve over the cream and mix the Armagnac into the custard. The custard is now ready.

Cut the buttered bread into triangular halves and arrange eight in the base of the dish. Top with half the soaked prunes and cover with just six slices of the bread. Scatter over the remaining prunes, arranging the final ten slices of bread slightly overlapping on top.

Pour over the warm custard, lightly pressing the bread down. Leave to stand for 20 to 30 minutes. Place the dish in a roasting tray and three quarters fill with warm water. Cover with buttered foil and bake for 20 to 30 minutes until just beginning to set. Remove the pudding from the tray and leave to stand for 10 to 15 minutes before sprinkling extra caster sugar liberally on top. Preheat the grill.

To glaze, pop under the grill and colour to a crunchy caramelized finish. A blowtorch can also be used to achieve the glazed finish.

serves six

175g (6oz) ready-to-eat prunes, halved
5 tablespoons Armagnac
12 medium slices of white bread, crusts cut off
50g (2oz) unsalted butter, softened
1 vanilla pod or a few drops of vanilla extract
400ml (14fl oz) double cream
400ml (14fl oz) milk
8 egg yolks
175g (6oz) caster sugar, plus extra for glazing

blackberry clafoutis

This recipe is more or less fruit baked in a sweet Yorkshire pudding batter. The batter can be flavoured with lemon or orange zest or a flavoured liqueur, such as amaretto with its almond edge or perhaps the blackberry liqueur, crème de mure. The pudding can be cooked in one round ovenproof dish large enough for four portions or four individual dishes.

Preheat the oven to 180°C/350°F/gas 4.

Whisk together in a large bowl the eggs and sugar. Sift the flour over the mix and whisk in well before stirring in the cream and milk. Leave the batter to rest for 10 minutes before baking.

Lightly butter a baking dish and sprinkle with caster sugar to coat. Scatter the blackberries in the dish, gently pouring the sweet batter over the fruits.

Bake for 20 to 25 minutes until the batter is just firm to the touch. If it is still too soft in the centre, bake for a further 5 minutes. Remove the clafoutis from the oven and allow to cool slightly before serving.

more
- *A dollop of extra-thick cream on top would be perfect.*
- *The clafoutis can be sprinkled lightly with extra caster sugar once baked and placed beneath the grill, glazing and giving a slightly bitter, burnt edge.*

serves four

2 large eggs
75g (3oz) caster sugar, plus
  extra for dusting
40g (1½oz) plain flour
100ml (3½fl oz) double
  cream or crème fraîche
100ml (3½fl oz) milk
butter, for greasing
225g (8oz) blackberries

apple tart

This recipe is based on the classic French apple tart, with blackberry jam spread over the tart base to provide a bit more of a British touch.

Preheat the oven to 200°C/400°F/gas 6. Lightly grease and flour a 23–25cm (9–10 inch) loose-bottomed tart ring.

Roll out the pastry on a lightly floured surface into a circle large enough to line the tart tin. Lift the pastry on the rolling pin and place in the tart tin, easing the pastry into the bottom and corners of the tin. Prick the base well with a fork. Refrigerate for 20 minutes.

Meanwhile, peel and core six of the apples and cut each into thin wedges or chunks. Sprinkle with a little lemon juice, mixing it through well. Place the apples and sugar in a saucepan over a medium to low heat. Cook for 12 to 15 minutes, stirring occasionally until tender. Spoon the apples into a colander or sieve to drain off any liquid.

Line the pastry case with greaseproof paper. Fill with baking beans or rice and blind bake for 15 minutes. Remove the paper and beans and return the tart case to the oven for a further 5 minutes. Remove from the oven and leave to cool. Once cool, spread the blackberry jam over the base of the tart.

Reduce the oven temperature to 190°C/375°F/gas 5.

Peel, core and very thinly slice the remaining apples, squeezing over a few dots of lemon juice. Spread the softened apples into the tart case. Arrange the raw apple slices on top in a circular fashion and bake for 25 to 30 minutes. Leave the tart to cool slightly before removing from the tin. The tart can be served warm or cold and dusted lightly with icing sugar, if using.

serves six–eight

275–350g (10–12oz) ready-made sweet shortcrust pastry
9 firm, crisp eating apples
a squeeze of lemon juice
25g (1oz) caster sugar
3 heaped tablespoons blackberry (or blackcurrant) jam
icing sugar, for dusting (optional)

baked amaretti peaches

After experiencing something very similar to this in Italy, this baked peaches recipe just had to be included. A dollop of extra-thick cream melting over the top is heavenly, but I've also included a recipe for an amaretto zabaglione to drizzle over – purely optional.

Preheat the oven to 180°C/350°F/gas 4.

Halve the peaches and remove the stones. Put the amaretti biscuits in a bag and crush with a rolling pin. Mix the crushed biscuits in a bowl with the amaretto, ground almonds, egg yolks and sugar.

Fill each of the peach halves with the almond mix, completely covering the surface with a smooth even finish. Top each peach with a small knob of butter and place on a greased non-stick baking tray. Bake for 20 to 25 minutes or until the peaches are completely tender. Dust lightly with icing sugar just before serving.

Meanwhile, whisk together the egg yolks, sugar, amaretto and 50ml (2fl oz) water in a large bowl. Ten minutes before the peaches are ready, place the bowl over a pan of gently simmering water. Using a balloon whisk or electric hand whisk, whisk for 8 to 10 minutes until the zabaglione has thickened to a creamy, whipped meringue stage. Remove the bowl from the heat and the zabaglione is ready to drizzle over the peaches.

serves four

4 peaches
75g (3oz) amaretti biscuits
2 tablespoons amaretto
   (sweet sherry can be used)
50g (2oz) ground almonds
2 egg yolks
3 teaspoons caster sugar
25g (1oz) butter
icing sugar, for dusting

for the zabaglione
4 egg yolks
75g (3oz) caster sugar
75ml (3fl oz) amaretto

hazelnut cake with frangelico cream

Preheat the oven to 180°C/350°F/gas 4. Line an 18cm (7 inch) loose-bottomed cake tin with buttered grease-proof paper.

Grind the hazelnuts finely in a food processor to a ground almond stage. Put the digestive biscuits in a plastic bag and crush with a rolling pin. Using an electric mixer, beat together the butter and sugar until creamy.

Sift the self-raising flour into a bowl and mix together with the ground hazelnuts and crushed digestive biscuits. Slowly add the dry mix into the creamy butter, followed by one egg at a time, until all totally combined and smooth.

Spoon the cake mix into the tin, smoothing the top. Bake in the oven for 25 to 30 minutes until the cake is just beginning to come away from the sides of the tin and is golden brown and firm in the middle. Take out of the oven and leave to cool before removing from the tin. The cake can be served cold or each slice lightly warmed in the microwave.

To make the Frangelico cream, pour the cream into a bowl along with the icing sugar and Frangelico. Whip to a light soft peak stage and dollop on top of the cake slices.

more
- *Some extra whole hazelnuts can be roasted in a frying pan to a rich golden brown and used to garnish the cake (or roughly chop and sprinkle over the cream).*
- *A warm chocolate sauce drizzled over the top of the cake could be delicious. Put 100g (4oz) chopped dark chocolate and 150ml (5fl oz) double cream in a bowl and place over a pan of gently simmering water or microwave. Once the chocolate is melted, remove the bowl from the heat or microwave and stir until silky smooth, adding a small knob of butter for an even more glossy finish.*

serves four–six

for the hazelnut cake
150g (5oz) skinned hazelnuts
25g (1oz) digestive biscuits
175g (6oz) butter
100g (4oz) caster sugar
    (golden caster, if available)
25g (1oz) self-raising flour
3 eggs

for the Frangelico cream
150ml (5fl oz) double cream
1 heaped tablespoon icing
    sugar
3 tablespoons Frangelico

iced jersey cream with lots of strawberries

This is purely an ice cream made from Jersey cream and milk.

Bring the milk and cream to the boil

Meanwhile, beat the egg yolks and sugar together until thick and creamy. Pour the boiled milk into the mix, whisking continuously, then pour the custard mix back into the saucepan and stir continuously. Cook over a low heat until the custard thickens, coating the back of a spoon.

Remove the custard from the heat and leave to cool before churning in an ice-cream machine until thickened and frozen.

Whiz 150g (5oz) of the strawberries with the jam in a blender until smooth, adding a teaspoon or two of icing sugar to sweeten, if needed. Strain the sauce through a sieve.

The iced Jersey cream, strawberries and strawberry sauce are ready to scoop and drizzle into bowls.

more
- *To accompany? Perhaps the shortbread biscuits on page 242.*
- *If an ice-cream machine is unavailable, simply freeze the mixture in a bowl, stirring from time to time until completely frozen. For a creamier finish, place the ice-cream in a food processor and blitz until smooth. Pour back into the bowl and re-freeze until set.*

serves four–six

300ml (10fl oz) full-fat Jersey milk
300ml (10fl oz) Jersey cream
6 egg yolks
150g (5oz) caster sugar

for the strawberry sauce
650g (1½lb) strawberries, hulled
1 tablespoon strawberry jam
icing sugar, to taste

chocolate and cherry pie

This pastry pie is filled here with a chocolate and almond sponge. Cherries have also been added, using tinned syrup or alcohol-based morello cherry varieties. The chocolate almond sponge is mixed with pastry cream before baking in the pastry.

To make the pastry cream, put the milk in a saucepan with the scraped vanilla pod and seeds and bring to the boil. Mix together the egg yolks, sugar and flour and pour on the hot milk, whisking to combine. Return the mixture to the saucepan and cook gently over a low heat, stirring continuously until thickened. Strain through a sieve into a bowl, cover and leave to cool.

Put all the chocolate almond sponge ingredients, bar the chopped chocolate and cherries, into a food processor and blitz until smooth. Stir in the chilled pastry cream, chopped chocolate and halved cherries and refrigerate until firm.

Preheat the oven to 200°C/400°F/gas 6.

Unroll the puff pastry sheets. These can be left in their rectangular shape or lightly rolled and each cut into 25–28cm (10–11 inch) discs. Place one of the pastry sheets or discs on parchment paper on a baking tray.

Spread the chocolate mixture onto the centre of the pastry sheet or disc, creating a slight dome and leaving a 2.5cm (1 inch) border all the way around. Brush around the border with the beaten egg.

Top the chocolate mixture with the remaining pastry, pressing down firmly around the border. Brush with the beaten egg and bake for 35 to 40 minutes until golden and crispy. Dust with icing sugar and serve with the pouring cream.

more
• *The pie can also be served just warm or cold.*

serves six–eight

for the pastry cream
250ml (9fl oz) milk
1 vanilla pod, split lengthways and the seeds scraped out
3 egg yolks
75g (3oz) caster sugar
25g (1oz) plain flour

for the chocolate almond sponge
100g (4oz) butter
100g (4oz) caster sugar
2 eggs
100g (4oz) ground almonds
50g (2oz) cocoa powder
75g (3oz) plain chocolate, roughly chopped
75g (3oz) cherries (see left), halved

2 x sheets of fresh ready-rolled puff pastry
1 egg, beaten
icing sugar, to dust
cream, to serve

poached nutty meringues

Toasted almonds enhance these sweet, light meringues. They need only to be served with a fresh custard (sauce anglaise – a French classic to accompany poached meringues), of which there are plenty to choose from in most supermarkets. I'm including strawberries with their own sauce here (also used to accompany the iced Jersey cream on page 237). They are totally optional, with plenty of other seasonal fruits to choose from throughout the year.

In an electric mixer, whisk the egg whites to a soft peak. Add a tablespoon of the sugar and whisk, continuing in this fashion until all of the sugar is used up and the meringue has reached a smooth firm peak stage.

Meanwhile, warm the milk with an equal quantity of water in a large saucepan to just below simmering (70–80°C). Shape the meringues between two large kitchen spoons or form simple rustic dollops, creating enough for one, two or three meringues per person, whatever you prefer.

Poach the meringues in the milk for a few minutes before carefully turning. Continue to poach for a further few minutes before removing using a draining spoon and placing on parchment paper. Leave to cool. The meringues are best eaten just warm or at room temperature.

Meanwhile, preheat the grill. Scatter the flaked almonds on a baking tray and toast until golden brown.

Arrange a pile of strawberries on each of the plates and drizzle liberally with the strawberry sauce. Put the meringues next to the strawberries, inserting the toasted almonds into them to create a 'hedgehog' look and offering the custard in a small jug or bowl.

serves six–eight

for the meringues
4 egg whites
225g (8oz) caster sugar
300ml (10fl oz) milk
12–15 flaked almonds per person
fresh vanilla custard (see left)

1 x strawberry sauce (optional – see page 237)

raspberry and white chocolate cream shortbreads

This dessert can be simply presented with the raspberries, white chocolate cream and shortbreads all sat side by side. However, here I'm topping a couple of shortbread biscuits with the fruit and cream and stacking in a millefeuille style.

To make the shortbreads, cream together the butter, icing sugar and egg yolk. Sift the flour into the bowl and gently fold in with your fingertips. Roll into a cylinder, clingfilm and refrigerate for 1 to 2 hours.

Preheat the oven to 180°C/350°F/gas 4.

Once rested, roll the dough until just 2–3mm (1/8 inch) thick. Twelve circles, squares or rectangles can now be cut and placed on a non-stick baking tray. Bake for 12 to 15 minutes or until the shortbreads are lightly golden. Leave to cool.

Spoon or pipe the white chocolate cream onto eight of the shortbreads, leaving a 5–10mm (1/4–1/2 inch) border. Arrange the raspberries around the cream. Stack the shortbreads into four portions, finishing with the remaining shortbreads.

more
- *If you fancy a raspberry sauce to go with this, whiz 100g (4oz) raspberries and 25g (1oz) icing sugar in a blender until smooth. Strain through a sieve and serve.*

serves four

1 x white chocolate
  cream (see page 213),
  refrigerated for 10 to 15
  minutes before using
20–24 raspberries per person

for the shortbreads
200g (7oz) butter, softened
100g (4oz) icing sugar
1 egg yolk
250g (9oz) plain flour

passion fruit mousse

To make the mousse, cut the passion fruit in half and scoop out the flesh. Blitz the flesh in a food processor or using a handheld blender until all of the flesh and juice have been removed from the seeds. Push the juice through a fine sieve using a large spoon.

Bring the milk up to the boil in a saucepan. Meanwhile, whisk together the egg yolks and sugar to a thick, pale cream. Whisk the hot milk into the egg yolks and return the custard to the saucepan. Gently heat to thicken, stirring continuously until the mixture begins to coat the back of the spoon. Strain and set aside to cool.

Gently heat the passion fruit juice and add the gelatine, stirring until dissolved. Pour into the custard and stir well. Set aside to cool, allowing the mix to slowly thicken while it cools. Whip the cream to a peak and slowly introduce into the custard, folding in until fully mixed together. Pour the mousse slowly into a serving bowl so as not to create too many air bubbles. Leave to cool and set for 2 to 3 hours on an even surface in the fridge.

For the passion fruit jelly, follow the same method to make the juice. In a small saucepan, warm the juice, sugar and 100ml (3½fl oz) water and simmer until the sugar has dissolved. Remove from the heat and stir in the gelatine. Once totally cooled, pour the jelly over the chilled mousse. Refrigerate for a further 1 to 2 hours to set.

For the passion fruit sauce, follow the same method to make the juice, saving the seeds from one or two fruit. Gently heat the sugar and 80ml (3fl oz) water and once the sugar has dissolved, remove from the heat and stir in the juice. If it's too thin, the sauce can be returned to the boil, allowing it to evaporate and reduce to a thicker consistency. Stir in the seeds and leave to cool. Serve the mousse drizzled with the sauce.

serves six–eight

for the passion fruit mousse
12 passion fruit, to yield approximately 200ml (7fl oz) juice (or make up with fresh smooth orange juice)
300ml (10fl oz) full-fat milk
4 egg yolks
75g (3oz) caster sugar
3 leaves of gelatine, soaked in cold water
250ml (9fl oz) double cream

for the passion fruit jelly
6 passion fruit, to yield approximately 150ml (5fl oz) juice
25g (1oz) caster sugar
3 leaves of gelatine, soaked in cold water

for the passion fruit sauce
6 passion fruit, to yield approximately 150ml (5fl oz) juice
25g (1oz) caster sugar

risotto rice pudding with cognac golden sultanas

This rice pudding is made with arborio rice, hence its title. The method is very much that of a classic rice pudding, simmering the rice gently in milk and cream until it has swelled and become tender and creamy. The golden sultanas are warmed in the Cognac and stirred in, and the dish is finished off with a knob of butter, just as you would a risotto.

Put the sultanas and brandy in a small saucepan and gently bring to a simmer. Remove the pan from the heat and keep to one side.

Pour the milk and cream into a saucepan and add the grated orange zest and vanilla pod. Bring to the boil before adding the rice and sugar. Simmer gently over a low heat, stirring slowly, for 30 to 35 minutes until the rice is completely cooked through and creamy.

Remove the vanilla pod from the rice and stir in the soaked sultanas. Add the knob of butter and the 'risotto' is ready to serve.

more
- *The rice pudding can be served hot or cold. If cold, accompany with a fresh orange segment salad for a more refreshing taste.*

serves four

75g (3oz) golden sultanas
3–4 tablespoons Cognac
700ml (1¼ pints) milk
300ml (10fl oz) double cream
finely grated zest of 1 small
   orange
1 vanilla pod, split
   lengthways
100g (4oz) arborio rice
50g (2oz) caster sugar
a large knob of butter

index

acknowledgements

There are so many members of the 'Rhodes Team' that I would like to thank, and many others as well who I haven't the space to include here, but deserving an extra special mention are:

Camilla Stoddart. A truly brilliant lady to work with, here's a huge thank you. We are all going to miss you.

Lissanne Kenyon. The best PA in the world – just how do you put up with me?!

Wayne Tapsfield. For working on yet another book and looking after Rhodes W1 Restaurants and many more . . .

Adam Gray. Head chef at Rhodes Twenty Four restaurant, for maintaining such an honourable Michelin star level.

Lisa Harrison, Sarah Tildesley and Lucida Kaizik. For trying, testing and tasting every single dish featured in this book.

Tom Weldon. For believing in Rhodes recipes.

John Hamilton. An art director with such vision and a 'foodie' who more than appreciates good flavours.

Kay Halsey. For making sure I don't waffle with my words.

Lottie Davies. The photographer, for keeping all of these recipes alive.

Chris Callard. The designer of the book.

All at Penguin who have worked so hard to make this book a success.

And, of course, special thanks to the lady I've loved for over thirty years, my wife Jennie, and our two amazing sons, Samuel and George.